Danger
in the
Comfort
Zone

Danger in the Comfort Zone

From Boardroom to
Mailroom—How to
Break the Entitlement
Habit That's Killing
American Business

Judith M. Bardwick

American Management Association

New York • Atlanta • Boston • Chicago • Kansas City • San Francisco • Washington, D. C.
Brussels • Mexico City • Tokyo • Toronto

This book is available at a special
discount when ordered in bulk quantities.
For information, contact Special Sales Department,
AMACOM, a division of American Management Association,
135 West 50th Street, New York, N.Y. 10020.

Library of Congress Cataloging-in-Publication Data

Bardwick, Judith M., 1933–
    Danger in the comfort zone : from boardroom to mailroom—how to
break the entitlement habit that's killing American business /
Judith M. Bardwick.
      p.   cm.
    Includes bibliographical references and index.
    ISBN 0-8144-7886-7
    1. Psychology, Industrial—United States.   2. Work—Psychological
aspects.   3. Entitlement attitudes—United States.   4. Employees—
United States—Attitudes.   5. Job security—United States.
6. Labor productivity—United States.   I. Title.
HF5548.8.B243   1995
158.7—dc20   94-24020
                                              CIP

Printing number

10 9 8 7 6 5 4 3 2 1

This book is dedicated to
Rachel Elizabeth Ahearn
from her adoring grandmother.

Contents

Author's Note

Throughout this book I recount many stories of success and failure, of companies large and small, of people who feel energized by their work and those who feel terribly afraid.

Most of those that involve actual companies are taken from business periodicals and are so identified in each chapter's references (see pages 235ff.). In these cases, where names of companies and company leaders are given, they are the real names.

Stories not cited with a reference are the result of interviews I conducted with businesspeople in various industries. Quotations unattributed to a published source should be presumed to be from such interviews.

Still other stories are fictionalized accounts, inspired by real people with whom I am acquainted in one way or another but whose names are disguised.

Acknowledgments

I'd like to acknowledge the help given to me and express my thanks to the following special people:

To my literary agent, Barbara Hogensen of the Lucy Kroll Agency, for her marvelous competency.

To Adrienne Hickey, AMACOM's Senior Acquisitions Editor, for her piercing intelligence combined with powerful enthusiasm.

To my friends, venture capitalist Tom Murphy, and Norman Schoenfeld, President of Elco Corporation, who, early on, understood the theme and contributed wisdom and examples from their experience.

To Judy Taub of IBM in Poughkeepsie, who created the graphics as an unexpected and wonderful present.

To Bill Bryan, Program Manager; Tom Schappert, Manager, Management Development Programs; Ed Brewington, Director of Management Education, IBM Corporation, USA; and all at the IBM Management Development Center for their encouragement and commitment as the theme of this book has become part of the center's curriculum.

To the people at AMACOM, and my friends, Linda and Jack Finkelstein, Gary and Linda Eaton, Tom Murphy (again!), and Lee Doyle and Marita Sullivan, all of whom helped to create the title of the book.

To my daughter and first editor, Deborah Susan Bardwick, who thrilled me by clearly demonstrating greater writing skills than mine.

To free-lance editor Marty Stuckey of Portland, Oregon, who earlier edited *The Plateauing Trap,* and who created an even greater miracle with the manuscript of *this* book.

To my partner and husband, Captain Allen E. Armstrong, U.S. Coast Guard, Retired, who, more than anyone, contributes both indirectly and directly to all that I achieve.

To all of you, my heartfelt thanks!

A Note to the Reader

Dear Reader,

Danger in the Comfort Zone was first published in October 1991. That's not so very long ago in absolute terms and is really a very short time considering the magnitude of the changes that have occurred since then in many parts of the world, including the United States in 1991, *Danger* referred to the widespread Entitlement mentality that had developed because many people had too much security, especially job security. While the legacy of Entitlement is still very much with us, now *Danger* has come to have a very different meaning. In just these few years, many people in many nations have gone from having too little risk at work to having too much. They are in the state described as fear—the opposite end of the continuum.

We have all kinds of fashionable words: *reinventing, reengineering, downsizing, rightsizing, delayering* . . . these are euphemistic terms coined to make a hard message easier to take. These words reflect the increasing pressure on most organizations, in the majority of nations, in the private sector, and even to some smaller extent in government, to cut costs and become vastly more efficient. For those still employed, there are fewer promotions and many more early retirements than there were at the start of most careers. And many who expected security are now unemployed.

At the core of what is happening, the implicit employment contract that many people took for granted is either in grave jeopardy or it's gone. Not long ago, people joined an organization where they'd likely spend their whole career. But "the contract" wasn't just about knowing *where* you'd work. Unstated but understood by everyone who worked in large corporations, powerful unions, hospitals, governments, and school systems was *the deal*. The basic agreement between the employee and the organization was that if you didn't screw things up too badly and your loyalty was obvious, between your salary when you worked and your pension when you didn't you were safe because the organization took care of you as long as you lived.

But times have changed, and they've changed big time. Security has been replaced by insecurity. Individuals who never had to deal with much risk now have to cope with an unpredictable and very serious reality. And organizations are discovering that they must redefine and redesign *commitment* because organizations no longer have unilateral control over what happens to them—and therefore they can't make long-term promises to people.

Welcome to the future.

The model and the concepts of *Danger in the Comfort Zone* are as valid and as useful as they were when the book was first published. But in light of the changes I've just described, the focus has shifted so that Fear has become much more important.

Despite this change, the legacy of Entitlement remains extremely difficult to uproot. Even while we have powerful amounts of fear, anxiety, and anger, we still must deal with the Entitlement mentality and the bureaucratic structure embedded in many of our organizations.

The last five chapters of this paperback edition of *Danger in the Comfort Zone* offer additional ways to attack the problem—going beyond the methods described in the original text and recognizing the climate of today's business environment. They will also give you a foretaste of my next book, now in the development stage and tentatively entitled *Find Comfort in Endless Danger*. That's what's become permanent . . . and real.

This new edition of *Danger in the Comfort Zone* also includes updated facts and figures throughout.

Last, but definitely not least, while Entitlement is still a core part of our culture, especially in government and education, our corporations have been making significant progress. I am, therefore, encouraged. In fact, I've become cautiously optimistic.

I hope you enjoy the new material.

Sincerely,

JMB

April 1995

Introduction

A New Look at a Familiar Problem

America no longer strides across the economic landscape as though she owned it. Our dominance is declining. We know it and we dislike it. All kinds of experts explain it: Politicians point to unfair trade practices, economists talk about the high cost of money, and engineers cite inefficient production techniques. But since this is a book by a psychologist, we're going to look at psychological causes.

Why is our productivity sagging? One reason rarely mentioned is that for many people the work ethic no longer shines as brightly as it used to. Too many Americans no longer work as hard or as well as they should. Even when people put in a lot of time, they don't accomplish much. They don't add value.

Employers unwittingly perpetuate this attitude by their failure to hold people accountable for doing good work. They don't really expect people to excel, so evaluating performance is a half-hearted exercise at best.

For the past twelve years I have spent most of my time as a consultant for some of the largest U.S. companies. As I observed the daily workings of more and more organizations, I found one consistent characteristic: Too many people put in "face time." They show up for work, and think that's good enough. Many even believe they're working hard. Most believe they're contributing.

For example, one company convened a committee of fifteen people from six different states to see how career plateauing—the lack of promotion opportunity—was affecting morale. I was asked to work with the group because I'd already given more than ten workshops on plateauing to its middle managers. In fact, half the committee members had been in those workshops.

"Our mission," the members told me, "is to find out how people feel about plateauing."

"But you already know," I protested. "You've been to the workshops yourselves. And you have heaps of survey data. It's your number one problem."

"We have to be sure," they said.

So the committee met for another year. Every six weeks or so, the members would leave their jobs and convene at headquarters to discuss a question they already had the answer to.

What's going on? U.S. corporations are run by some of the smartest people in the world. How could we have gotten to the point where workers are allowed to spend their time in such nonproductive ways? What has happened to our expectation that people should earn a real salary by doing real work? What happened to the Yankee notion that you ought to earn what you get?

This is what happened: The United States was so rich for so long that we no longer asked people to earn promotions, raises, and security. We stopped doing the work of requiring real work. As it turned out, we gave too much security to too many people. It wasn't good for our institutions and it wasn't good for our people. The dynamics we're talking about can be seen just as clearly in other relationships between people, especially in families.

Three years ago I was involved in a lengthy project for a major oil company. Over time, I developed friendships with several of the managers, including one middle manager in his forties. Even though his annual salary was somewhere around $50,000, he was always broke. A guilty divorced father, he spent about 40 percent of his income supporting his daughter. While the father was poor, the daughter was rich—private school, private tennis lessons, ritzy summer camp, and so forth.

One morning he pulled me aside, obviously upset, saying "I have to talk to you."

"Sure," I said. "What's up?"

"It's my daughter. I got a call from her last night."

"And?"

"And she said she called to remind me that I owe her a car."

"You *owe* her a car?"

"Yeah."

"Did she say *why* you owe her a car?"

"Because she's about to turn sixteen. She says I owe her a car because she's sixteen."

In that moment I "saw" the psychology of Entitlement.

What Is Entitlement?

Entitlement is the name I have given to an attitude, a way of looking at life. Those who have this attitude believe that they do not have to earn what they get. They come to believe that they get something because they are owed it, because they're *entitled* to it. They get what they want because of *who* they are, not because of what they *do*.

Entitlement is what I have been seeing in American corporations: people not really contributing, but still expecting to get their regular raise, their scheduled promotion. When this rich nation stopped requiring performance as a condition for keeping a job or getting a raise, it created a widespread attitude of Entitlement. Entitlement destroys motivation. It lowers productivity. In the long run it crushes self-esteem. And despite the layoffs of recent years, it is epidemic in this country. It's our legacy of the boom times that followed World War II.

The psychology of Entitlement is a concept. Using that concept, I have developed a very simple and very powerful model. In psychology, a model is a way of looking at relationships. The model is a lens, a tool to see familiar issues in a new way. It explains a lot of what is happening to us, and provides a clear perception of what we must do. My experience with using the model in business leads me to feel confident that it is a useful contribution in our drive for enhanced performance.

The Architecture of This Book

This book seeks to examine the collective body of American business, diagnosing unhealthy conditions and prescribing healthy alternatives. Its fundamental aim is to present a new perspective on the causes of our ailing productivity.

Chapter 1 sets the stage by briefly recounting economic trends since World War II and the attitudes that developed in our companies and among our workers during two main periods: the prosperous times just after the war and the downward cycle starting in the early 1970s.

Chapters 2 through 4 describe three psychological states and show what those states look like in organizations.

Entitlement:	People are complacent; they get raises, bonuses, and benefits pretty much as a matter of course, so there is no incentive to work hard.
Fear:	People are analyzed; the threat of layoffs makes them focus on *protecting* their jobs rather than *doing* them.
Earning:	People are energized by challenge; they know their work will be judged and that rewards will be based on accomplishment.

In these chapters we begin to see an inevitable progression. The economic environment of the larger marketplace creates a psychological environment in a particular organization that in turn controls people's attitudes toward their jobs.

Chapter 5 pulls the three psychological conditions together into one visual presentation called the Earning Curve. This graphic makes clear the dynamic flow from one condition to another, and shows the relationship between psychological state and productivity level. When put into the form of a graph, the idea becomes stunningly simple.

Chapters 6 through 8 help senior executives and managers develop a strategy for improving productivity by changing the psychological environment of their companies, thus moving from the lethargy of Entitlement or the paralysis of Fear to the vigor of Earning. Chapter 9 coalesces the strategies into a description of the dynamics of change and focuses the spotlight on key features of the new paradigm.

Most of this book will be directed toward business, but the model that will unfold has many applications. In Chapter 10, we look at the psychology of Entitlement from a personal level. Entitlement is at its core a very simple idea, but its very simplicity begets lots of questions. Chapter 11 is a collection of the questions I am most commonly asked when I present seminars and workshops on Entitlement issues in organizations.

The Task Ahead

Historically, rich organizations in a rich nation were willing to be "nice" and carry even those who didn't add value. In large bureaucracies, it was also easy to hide, which made it even more likely that people would not be held accountable for real work. Over time, everyone who is not held accountable has all the time in the world.

In organizations where there is no sense of urgency, morale and motivation are usually very low. There's no vitality, no energy. And what of the people who work in those organizations? At first, such total security seems wonderful. But before long, a kind of heavy complacency settles in. When the system is unresponsive, when the organization does not require work that makes a difference, when outstanding performers are not rewarded for their accomplishments, and when underachieving performers are not punished, people become apathetic. In organizations where nothing much happens regardless of whether you do something exceptional or just show up in the morning, the best people lose heart and motivation is reduced near the lowest common denominator.

The task that faces this nation is a move from a psychology of Entitlement to one of Earning. But that will take great courage, because leaving Entitlement requires a sojourn into the psychology of Fear. Holding the flashlight for that journey—leading the way from Entitlement through Fear to Earning—is the goal of this book.

Part One

Danger in the Comfort Zone

1

The American Dream Shattered

Generation after generation of Americans have climbed up the economic ladder, each standing higher than the one before it. The American Dream is based on a contract that says, "If you work hard, you are going to be more successful than your parents were." Those born in the Depression years found themselves, after the war, with opportunities and resources their parents had never imagined. Their children, the baby boomers, grew up with even higher expectations of success.

The same economic trends that realized that dream for an extraordinary number of people also spawned a certain way of thinking. In American companies, an attitude of Entitlement developed in both the organizations themselves and among the people who worked in them. What happened to the dream, and what happened to that way of thinking, is the focus of this chapter.

America the Prosperous

The years after World War II offered more people the opportunity for success than ever before in the United States. The boom years lasted approximately from the end of the war in 1946 to the recession and oil embargo of 1973 (the exact dates vary for different industries and organizations). The fat times were created by four extraordinary conditions that occurred simultaneously.

The first was the growth rate of the economy. For more than twenty-five years, despite several recessions, the U.S. economy sustained its highest growth rate ever. After sixteen years of depression and war, we experienced an explosive growth in consumer demand.

The second was our dominance in the world economy. During all those years, we were simply the unquestioned leader.

The third variable was the incredibly high birth rate that began in 1946. In the eighteen years from 1946 to 1964, 76 million babies were born.

In combination with the high growth rate of the economy, the high birth rate created the fourth condition: the tremendous expansion in the size of companies and organizations. In the decades that followed the war, institutions grew at the highest rates the United States over experienced. In some companies, like AT&T, middle management grew by 500 percent. The 1950s and 1960s have been called "the Golden Age of the U.S. corporation."

Together, these four extraordinary conditions created unparalleled opportunities. And the people who could take advantage of those opportunities had been born in the 1920s and 1930s when the birth rate was the lowest in U.S. history. Thus, people who grew up during the Depression went to work at a time when the opportunity rate was at its highest.

Entitlement: The Legacy of Prosperity

On the surface, unlimited growth would seem to be a good thing. Companies are strong and profitable and people have no trouble finding good jobs, so everyone is secure and happy. But it is one of the premises of this book that it is possible to have too much of a good thing, that those years of prosperity have now backfired. Gradually, insidiously, prosperity created the crippling condition called Entitlement, where workers have no real incentive to achieve and managers have stopped doing the work of requiring real work. (The dynamics of Entitlement are discussed in Chapter 3.)

How did this happen? For most of its history, the United

States has honored a tradition of self-sufficiency; individuals have been expected to take care of themselves and to earn their way. But by the 1950s, we had become a nation that expected our society to provide for its citizens and we expected U.S. companies to take care of their employees. What changed?

The answer was both an economic and a psychological component. Economically, Entitlement comes from two forces at work in those incredible years after World War II: economic boom and demographic bust. With a limited pool of employees, rich organizations kept all their workers, no matter how well or how poorly they performed. In spite of this, business and industry flourished. Entitlement is a legacy of these years of affluence.

At that time, too, the social sciences gained new significance in the popular culture and there was a shift in our beliefs about behavior. Psychology, psychiatry, and sociology all try to analyze and explain why people behave as they do. As we focused on the reasons for incompetence or nonperformance, we ceased judging. When people's work falls off in the midst of a nasty divorce, for example, we hesitate before we burden them with criticism. It's very difficult to be judgmental when you understand the cause.

As a nation we came to a new understanding of human behavior, one that led us to tolerate low achievement while also enjoying a tremendous economic prosperity. We were so rich we could afford to be kind.

Under the double influence of their corporate compassion and their rich treasuries, in the postwar decades organizations began to grant job security without regard to how well people worked and how much they contributed. They stopped evaluating employees and discharging those who were nonproductive; they failed to hold people accountable for their performance.

This tolerance of nonperformance was especially obvious in the case of plateaued employees, those who had reached the upper limit of their productivity. They were not required to be productive; they were not dismissed for being unproductive. Instead, plateaued people were allowed to hang around, read the paper, and serve on insignificant committees, such as the

Christmas Party Committee, the Annual Picnic Committee, the Committee to Allocate Office Space.

There was an unarticulated agreement that plateaued people gave up the excitement of being in the mainstream of the business in return for the comfort and security of lying on the shelf until it was okay to retire. Thus, management no longer did the work of evaluating their performance.

Over time, that attitude originally directed toward plateaued workers spread to all employees. Organizations no longer expected to get performance from every employee all the time. In the affluent years, companies were doing so well they could afford to carry nonproductive people.

Despite the recent and ongoing ravages of downsizing, that trend continues today in many companies, boosted by changes in the law. Under the old common-law concept of employment at will, the company had all the power; managers could fire laggards on the spot. Today it is very difficult to fire someone without running the risk of legal counteraction. When organizations don't fire, they never get rid of unproductive people. They can't afford to have them in responsible positions, so they make up jobs for them where they can't do any harm. Therefore, organizations end up with lots of employees who don't produce and who keep their jobs just by showing up. If the organization is really fat, these people even get merit raises. It is this corporate tolerance for nonperformance that has generated the psychology of Entitlement in American companies.

The End of the Dream

By the 1950s and 1960s, our economic lead was so total it was inconceivable that it could change. But in the early 1970s, our seemingly invincible strength was hit with a series of economic blows: the recession and oil embargo of 1973; the inflation and stagnation that followed; the recession of 1979; the recession of 1981–1982; and the stock market crash of October 18, 1987, Black Friday, when the Dow fell more than 500 points. In less than a generation, our nation went from feeling confident to feeling threatened.

The sons and daughters who assumed the American Dream from their parents are finding that for them the dream has begun to unravel. Hard work no longer guarantees upward mobility. No one anticipated what Paula Rayman of Wellesley calls "the middle-class squeeze—falling behind while getting ahead." As a group, the baby boomers are actually downwardly mobile. They're not able to live as well as adults as they did as kids. Richard Michel, an economist at the Urban Institute in Washington, D.C., says "The young middle class has experienced a dramatic decline in its ability to pursue the conventional American dream: a home, financial security, and education for their children." Lately, the average American has been running hard to stay in place.

The History of the New Business Reality

Something very fundamental has changed in economic realities. Productivity, which was growing at 4 percent a year, is now little more than 2 percent and is not rising. In February 1990, *Business Week* reported:

> Productivity in the U.S. has been in the doldrums for a long time—but now, its poor performance poses a threat to the economy. Output per hour in nonfarm industry rose at a paltry 1.2% annual rate in the 1980s—no improvement from the 1970s. Moreover, productivity heads into the 1990s at its slowest pace since the 1981–82 recession.
>
> For the coming year, poor productivity growth has a number of implications for the outlook—all bad.

We are the largest debtor nation in the world. The number of positions in our large corporations—white collar and blue collar—is declining. Previously immune to foreign competition, we are now unceasingly aware of it. Nations of the Pacific rim and Europe are lining up, competing for our markets, wooing our customers.

What this situation means for American companies is that they can no longer afford to perpetuate conditions of Entitlement. What that has meant for American workers is that companies can no longer afford to carry entitled, nonproductive people.

That's what led to the downsizings, restructuring, and reengineering of our corporations. It was necessary to increase our productivity rates significantly, and that's what happened. Productivity grew by the anemic rate of 0.9 percent in the 1980s, and averaged a measly 1 percent in the 1970s and 1980s. *Fortune* expects productivity to grow by 1.7 percent in 1994, and Alan Greenspan, chairman of the Federal Reserve is hoping it will continue to grow at 2 percent, the average of productivity increases since mid-1990.

Why is it really necessary to get high levels of productivity from everyone? One of the key answers is the shift to a global economy. A global economy is one in which you no longer have *your* customers. Companies can come from your own country, a neighboring country, or a country on the other side of the world in search of your customers.

With air travel there is no distance, there is only time. And sometimes there is no time. Communication by phone and fax is instantaneous. You can talk anywhere and deal anywhere instantly. And so can your competitors. In combination with increasing deregulation, the immediate result of this technology is that you have to fight for, service, and please your customers, because they literally have all the choice in the world. In the end, the only one who can provide job security is the customer.

Drew Lewis, chairman of Union Pacific, is trying to get the railroad to be more responsive to customers. In a recent meeting, several hundred rail workers demanded guaranteed jobs. He told them, "If I promise you a lifetime job, what is that worth if we're not competitive? It's worth a deck chair on the *Titanic.*"

When the customer is the only source of security, then security has to be continuously earned. Therefore, in a fundamental way, organizations cannot promise security because they don't have it. Organizations have to earn security through performance. And so they must demand performance from their employees, those individuals who make up the organization. No organization can afford to carry unproductive people anymore. Cost cutting has dominated the defensive strategies of corporate survival in recent years. Stripping away euphemisms like *downsizing* and *reduction in force,* the reality is one of layoffs, even of productive people. Job security for many is gone or at risk.

Beginning in the early 1980s, even corporations that had never fired people began to do so. One estimate is that in the 1980s more than 1 million managers and professionals were cut from the corporate ranks. Another estimate is that the number may be as high as 2 million.

Later in the decade the rate of cuts increased, and 1989 and 1990 saw more cutbacks than ever. The actual numbers vary according to who's counting and how middle manager and white collar are defined, but one fairly recent count emphasizes the accelerating problem: 111,285 middle managers and executives lost their jobs in all of 1989; in the first quarter of 1990 alone, the number was 110,152. In 1990, announcements of corporate cuts occurred at twice the 1989 rate. This retrenchment is cutting deeply in the ranks of middle and top-level managers and is now occurring in a wide range of companies that had not been affected in the 1980s.

Even organizations like Eastman Kodak, Polaroid, Exxon, AT&T, and Xerox, which have always had policies that amounted to lifetime employment, have begun to push out people through early retirement and firings. Eastman Kodak did away with 10 percent of its work force when it cut 13,000 positions. Exxon reduced its staff at headquarters in New York from 1,400 to 320. Hewlett-Packard offered early retirement packages to 1,800 employees. By the beginning of 1988, General Motors had cut its white-collar labor force by 25 percent and announced a further cut of 25,000 for 1989. Xerox pared down by 20 percent in the 1980s and said another one-third of its management and administrative staffs would be cut in the early 1990s.

America's largest, most powerful, and wealthiest corporations continue to downsize as though the United States were still in a recession. The ten largest industrial corporations in 1993 included General Motors, Exxon, Ford Motor Company, Inter-

national Business Machines, General Electric, Mobil Corporation, Philip Morris, E.I. Dupont, Chevron Corporation, and
Texaco Incorporated. These ten firms account for more than
two-thirds of a trillion dollars annually, and they employ
1,273,517 people. That number of employees is down by
160,000 jobs from the start of the economic recovery in 1991.
With the exception of Ford, all of these companies trimmed
their payroll during a period when the economy was growing.
We find the same pattern in the Standard & Poor's 500, a much
broader sample than the thirty companies in the Dow Industri-
als. In 1993, we saw that the number of jobs in the S&P had
declined by 500,000 from 1991, during a period of economic
growth. In 1994, *Fortune* reported the trend was continuing:
Total employment among the 500 had fallen again for the ninth
straight year, from 11,802,133 to 11,546,647. Clearly, productivity rates have grown at the expense of job security.

In 1993, the Families and Work Institute found in a survey
of 3,400 workers that 42 percent had experienced downsizing
and 28 percent reported cuts in management in the preceding
year.

The private sector is not alone in the changes it faces. By
1983, it had become clear that the employment boom in the
public sector was also hard hit and had become an employment
bust. In the middle of 1980, the federal government employed
16,735,000 people. Two and a half years later, after the recession of 1981–82, it was down to 15,197,000. In many local and
state governments the declines have continued, some dramatically. During the recession, for example, the state of Michigan
cut its 70,000 employees by 10,000.

One thing that made all the costs especially hard to bear
was that after we recovered from the recession of 1981–82, the
rate of cuts increased. Major cuts took place in the mid-1980s,
when employment was high, interest rates were low, there was
little inflation, the stock market was strong, and the economy
was growing. This situation increased people's sense of vulnerability.

The same thing is happening now. Long after the recovery
of the 1990 recession, corporations are continuing the practice
of laying people off. Middle managers especially continue to be

vulnerable because reengineering and technology continue to make it possible to manage well without them. Middle management's primary purpose was to transmit information up to executives and then relay orders down to the troops. That work is now done better and more cheaply by computer networks and databases.

Stephen Roach is a member of the National Academy of Sciences group that recently studied productivity in the service sector. That study concluded that the job shakeout which began in manufacturing in the early 1980s was probably about two-thirds completed. In contrast, in the service sector the job cuts are only about one-third done. The next big downsizing will impact retailing, banks, insurance companies, and any other organizations in which electronic systems are now poised to do work that millions of clerks used to handle.

What makes the changes even more difficult is they are likely to be permanent. According to Robert Tomasko, nine significant trends created the accelerated rate of downsizing, despite the strength of our economy. In addition to the trends we have already discussed, the movement of many American companies overseas, where costs are lower, has contributed. Sharply falling energy and commodity prices, most clearly in oil, have required industry cost-cutting in the producing industries. Many industries that were formerly regulated are now deregulated. After initial growth phases, deregulated industries now face tremendous competition and competitive price cutting. They, too, need to cut overhead. We've seen an enormous number of mergers and acquisitions. And, lastly, if we follow Britain's footsteps and privatize some of our government functions,* we can predict also the loss of public jobs as the businesses cut costs in pursuit of profits.

All the factors that Tomasko has identified have very little to do with short-term business cycles. The implication is that the times have truly changed and the changes are permanent.

---

*The United States Office of Personnel Management has proposed that many of its 600,000 jobs, ranging from data processing to vehicle maintenance, be spun off into businesses.

The Changing Employment Contract

The contract of understanding and obligation between employers and employees has changed. Most of our organizations, but especially those that enjoyed decades of Entitlement, maintained a powerful and implicit contract with their employees. In exchange for unswerving loyalty and a level of commitment that entailed putting the company before family or self, you had a position for life. The company invested in you and took care of you and gave you a raise every year. You could count on it.

The contract is particularly important for middle managers. Traditionally, blue-collar workers were protected by their unions, but middle managers were protected by a strongly felt and very specific invisible contract that said:

> Take care of business and we'll take care of you. You don't have to be a star; just be faithful, obedient, and only modestly competent, and this will be your home as long as you want to stay. We may have to lay off blue-collar workers now and then, or even cut off some heads at the very top, but unless we are in the deepest kind of trouble you will remain on the payroll. You are Family.

The old contract developed when national economic growth was great and the working population was relatively small. Not only could organizations afford to develop long-range plans for their employees but it was in their best interests to do so. Organizations offered promotion and other work-related benefits as well as life insurance, pensions, wellness, recreation, and social programs. Along with these benefits came the implicit understanding that the employee would remain with the organization and that the organization would not fire or lay off the employee.

In the new contract, the organization no longer assumes that it will employ people for the whole of their career. Therefore, it is unwilling to take care of them. Instead of being taken care of, employees are increasingly expected to become self-managing. There will be less long-term development of skills and more buying of them. People will be valued more for present performance and less for historic loyalty.

Increasingly, organizations will ask of potential employees, What do you bring to the table now? What skills do you have that are a contribution now? As a result, organizations will compete in the recruitment of outstanding people not just at the entry level but at every level. Similarly, people will compete with each other for employment, not just at the beginning but over the whole course of their careers.

The United States is not the same place it was after World War II. Our economy is no longer bursting at the seams with exuberant growth. We have lost the psychological sense of being in the driver's seat. We can no longer presume our dominance or our wealth. Individuals are learning they may not be able to afford something, like a house, that they assumed they would have as a birthright. And the nation is learning that it, too, cannot afford everything.

2

When Organizations Are Too Comfortable—The Lethargy of Entitlement

In 1983, I received a call from a human resources executive in a major manufacturing corporation, a Fortune 100 company. The company had a reputation for never firing anyone; children followed their parents into the company. The executive who called said the company was concerned about the low numbers of women and minorities in management and asked me to design a one-day workshop that would examine the psychological issues underlying the numbers.

A committee of four people had already spent about a year on the project, reading, interviewing, observing, and meeting with consultants nationwide. After developing a workshop outline, I met with the committee members for a day and explained my recommendations for the workshop.

Several weeks later, I was asked to return for five more days to go over the workshop design in detail. The entire five-day discussion was tape recorded and a secretary spent weeks transcribing every word for later study. Still, the committee didn't compare my suggestions with those of other experts it had consulted and it made no suggestions for change.

A month and a half later I was asked back. The committee had hired someone to be in charge of the workshop and thought it would be a good idea to bring him up to speed. Even though everyone had access to the transcriptions of our earlier discussions, we spent a week going through the same material again.

Two months later, I received another call. The committee had decided to go forward with the workshop, but it wanted handouts. Could I return for a week to write an outline?

Three months after that, we did a week of pilot workshops. During this entire period there had not been a single modification to my original workshop design. Each day, all five members of the committee sat at the back of the room and wrote down everything that was said. They also collected evaluations from every participant, which were very high. They were very busy, but they didn't say anything and they didn't change anything. Nothing happened as a result of their work.

Months later, I was asked to return for more pilot workshops. Those same five people sat in the back of the room and took notes all day. Again, they collected evaluations. Again, the evaluations were very high. And that was the end of the project. The actual workshop never occurred.

The committee members had put two years into planning the event. Once we reached the point of *doing* something (instead of planning) they simply stopped working on it. Neither they nor anyone is higher management seemed to care about the enormous investment in developing a program that never took place. It was as if the task were to design a workshop; no one seemed to remember that the real task was to prepare more minority workers and women for management positions.

I felt as though I had fallen into Alice's rabbit hole and landed in a strange land. Everyone but me had known all along that we had been engaged in a conspiracy of play acting. They were playing at working. If you define working as achieving something, they were not working. They were busy looking busy. And the organization, because it did not say "That won't do," was in effect saying "That's fine."

This company is a classic case of an organization stuck in the state of Entitlement. Over the years, the company has grown accustomed to mediocre performance levels. Mediocre has become normal so that even today those five committee members and their bosses see nothing remarkable in having spent two years planning a one-day workshop that never happened. This phenomenal waste of time will not jeopardize anyone's job security.

Entitlement in American Organizations

"This company is just like one big family." Chances are, whenever you hear people say that, they're talking about a company that is stuck in Entitlement. They're commenting on the warm sense of belonging, but unconsciously they're also talking about not having to earn their place. In the family at work, as in the family at home, Entitlement means you belong and you benefit precisely because you belong.

Expressed simply, Entitlement is the result of too much generosity. We give people what they expect and we don't hold them accountable for meeting criteria of excellence. In business it commonly happens because managers are unwilling to do the work of requiring work. Frequently it's because they want to avoid discord and bad feelings. Very often it arises from pity: We don't hold people accountable for results because we don't think they can perform. Good performance, poor performance, or no performance are all treated the same. In the workplace, people feel entitled when they have so much security that they don't have to earn their rewards.

- They keep their jobs and collect their regular paychecks no matter whether they produce much or little.
- They get their annual raises regardless of their contribution during the year.
- They are promoted because they have the right amount of seniority, not because they have demonstrated their superior competence for the higher-level jobs.
- They receive a year-end bonus because it's the end of the year, not because they've made notable achievements.

When people don't have to earn what they get, they soon take for granted what they receive. The real irony is that they're not grateful for what they get. Instead, they want more. It is the terrible cycle of Entitlement.

It is inaccurate to think of these issues only in terms of lower-level workers. Entitlement often goes through the highest ranks to the executive level. That's what we see when large corporations (General Motors was one) freeze wages, lay workers off, and give executives big bonuses. The same thing happened in some of the savings and loans that were taken over by federal administrators: They were losing money like crazy, but they were giving top officers hefty bonuses. Too often, there are no market forces operating at the highest level—executives get perks and bonuses irrespective of company performance—so the company operates to primarily benefit those who run it.

Too Much Security

"I've worked here a long time and have done what you expected. I've earned my security." That is the working presumption of the majority of people who work in our various government bodies, in all levels of our schools, in our large and powerful unions, and in our nature and prosperous corporations. It amounts to total job security. Too much security is what Entitlement is all about.

Job Security

Some groups of people (schoolteachers, for example) have formal tenure. They set a precedent for others to successfully argue their right to have the same certainty. In recent years those precedents became transformed into court decisions so that it became legally difficult to fire employees.

Under the old common-law concept of employment at will, the company had all the power; managers could fire laggards on the spot. Today it is very difficult to fire someone without running the risk of legal counteraction. As of January 1989, courts in forty-six states have issued rulings that erode the doctrine of employment at will, and at least thirteen states now recognize a vague principle known as the covenant of good faith and fair dealing, which says that each judge is free to decide whether or not an employee was fired without adequate cause.

Employers cannot fire employees without reasonable cause—for example, a reduction in force, unauthorized absenteeism, misbehavior, or failure to perform. For lawyers, this is proving to be a major windfall: a typical wrongful discharge suit in California, for example, awards damages of $700,000 if the employer loses.

With legal restrictions on top of tenure systems on top of a longstanding culture of nonaccountability, entitled organizations find it practically impossible to get rid of a nonproductive employee, even if they were so inclined. Often acutely ineffective people aren't fired; they are praised and passed on to someone else.

Too much security first shows up in organizations in the evaluation system. Where job security is absolute, companies gradually become less and less rigorous in their performance evaluation. Especially when people have reached their career plateaus, distinguishing between them becomes less important. Wherever it's very hard to fire people, evaluations are useful only to identify people who should be promoted. They are irrelevant for identifying those who should be penalized, because firing, which is the truly significant punishment, is no longer available. Thus, even though the formal culture may say "Evaluate!" the operating culture says "Why bother?"

Then, security generalizes to other aspects of life in the organization. First there is total job security; then seeking security, playing it safe in all dimensions, takes over as the dominant mode of operation.

When Security Is Institutionalized

Over time, the organization's culture becomes an accumulation of hundreds of ways to achieve security and avoid mistakes. These means are informal at first, then formal, until eventually Entitlement is fully institutionalized. This is the truly insidious danger with Entitlement: It settles in everywhere, and becomes part of the mortar that holds the organization together. Here are some of the ways that entitled organizations institutionalize security:

- Informal tenure for everyone
- An appraisal system that has no real impact
- A promotion system that doesn't reflect individual merit
- An emphasis on precedent
- Lots and lots of rules
- Lots and lots of paper
- A compensation system that doesn't really reflect what people do
- Committees with no real authority
- Rewards for fine-tuners, and punishment for innovators
- A formal hierarchy in which differences in power dictate permissible behavior
- Talk about pushing power down without real empowerment or delegation
- Layers of people whose jobs are making sure no mistakes are being made

Rules, Bureaucracy, and Hierarchy

From a culture made up of informal ways to avoid risk, it's a very easy step to a formalized system of precise rules, regulations, and procedures telling people exactly what to do so they don't make a mistake. When confidence is low, people are more comfortable if they know the boundaries of what's okay and what's not. Rules exist to tell people what they cannot do.

In the 1950s and 1960s, there were far fewer rules than there are now. As Entitlement became more common, the number of rules increased. The Defense Department controls its 134,000 employees through 4,000 laws and 30,000 pages of regulations. The department's acquisition regulations take 1.2 million lines or enough to fill 600 books that are 300 pages long: There are 20 pages for Defense Department fruit cake, 15 pages for T-shirts, and 7 pages for pencils.

The old AT&T provided rules for every contingency. The manual of *Bell Systems Instructions* took up 24 feet of shelf space, and the *Operating Procedures* manual took a few dozen feet more. One section alone—"How to Properly Take an Order"—was more than 1,200 pages long!

Before long, rules come to have a life of their own. Knowing and following the regulations becomes the end in itself. The emphasis is more on how things are done and less on what is accomplished. People become preoccupied with "doing it right," which comes to mean "by the book." It becomes more important than "doing it best."

Organizations with lots of rules usually have lots of checkers to make sure the rules are being obeyed. Institutions with too much security thus tend to become more and more bureaucratic. They add layers of rules to ensure that mistakes are never made, and layers of people to ensure that the rules are explained, understood, updated, and followed.

Prior to 1981, General Electric was a prime example of a bureaucracy. In the area of finance there was an unceasing need for longer, more detailed financial reports. One business unit put out seven daily reports, one of which made a pile 12 feet high, with sales data on every product manufactured— hundreds of thousands of items. When Jack Welch took over as CEO (chief executive officer) of GE in April 1981, the focus on bureaucracy changed. Welch considers bureaucracy "evil," believing it threatens productivity because it encourages people to look at the company and its procedures rather than at customers and the competition. He says "This internal focus has wasted our time, wasted our energy, frustrated us, made us so mad some nights over some bureaucratic jackass boss that we'd punch a hole in the wall."

As they add layers, bureaucratic organizations tend to become increasingly hierarchical. Then the culture, too, becomes ever more hierarchical; people pay a lot of attention to the differences in power at the different rungs on the ladder. Psychologically, the ladder is very tall. Where hierarchical status is really important, power is distributed from the top down.

The Consequences of Top-Down Power

In this kind of atmosphere, what happens to the employees? What does this kind of environment do to people's attitude about themselves, about their bosses, and about their work?

Pseudowork

In entitled organizations people concentrate on what looks good. *Looking* good is more important than *doing* good. Over time, form supplants substance. The appearance of being busy is equal in value to actually achieving. Doing excellent staff work, writing reports, doing analyses, creating committees, and holding meetings are more important than competing successfully in the marketplace. People lose sight of what's important; they are rewarded for simply putting in time.

Entitled organizations create red tape, paperwork, and pseudowork. There are endless meetings where nothing happens and there is no follow-up. Thousands of hours are invested in writing reports that no one reads. People write ponderous memos "to the file," explaining why they took no action.

A friend of mine who is a ranking officer in the State Department tells the story of interviewing a civil servant who wanted to transfer from Washington to Paris.

"Tell me what you do," my friend asked.

"I write reports."

"No, tell me what you accomplish. What will the result of your work be?"

"That's a very upsetting question."

Passivity

In hierarchical organizations, where power comes from the top down, people look up and wait for orders. They pay close attention to the nuances of behavior from those with more power. They know there is an unwritten contract that says "If you behave, you'll be okay." No wonder people pay so much attention to knowing the rules, following the boss's lead, knowing the right people, never making errors rather than risking, trying, and innovating.

I am distressed at how passive these hierarchical organizations make people. Even though they may appear active, they are waiting. More than anything, they keep their eye on the boss, waiting to be told what to do.

I remember going to a meeting with the CEO of a Baby

Bell and his top aides. I'd been doing some work in the company and they wanted to hear my impressions. The CEO is a smart and jovial man. He welcomed me with huge gestures of enthusiasm to his enormous boardroom table. Despite the hugging welcome, I sat alone at one end and he sat a football field away at the other end. His top people sat at his end, but not anywhere near his chair. The people who had brought me into the organization were not in the topmost group. They sat away from the table, flat against the wall.

"Judy," the CEO said, "I want you to tell me the truth. Tell me what you saw. Don't hold anything back!"

"Sure," I said. "Of course."

He leaned back. I started to talk. He interrupted. We listened to him. His aides elaborated on what he said. We all looked at him. He talked again. We continued looking at him. I tried to interject. He kept on talking. We kept on looking at him. He kept on talking. After thirty minutes I interrupted. "You asked me to tell you what I've seen. If you want me to tell you, you have to let me talk."

The room got dead quiet. No one looked at me. Everyone looked at the CEO. He made up his mind. He laughed. He said, "Okay. You're right. I'll shut up."

In that psychologically hierarchical organization, the CEO thought he was a democratic leader, a person who practiced participative management, who went out of his way to invite input from others. But the culture was so pervasively hierarchical, his right to be the authority was so ingrained, and it wasn't possible for him to notice that he always told and never listened. Formal or hierarchical authority is so basic to that institution that attempts to empower people and get them to be initiating must remain impotent and superficial until the culture is thoroughly transformed.

In bureaucratic, hierarchical organizations, nobody makes waves. I call them Country Club places. No one disagrees with anyone else in a substantive way. Asked an opinion, they'll check with the boss, swiftly agree, or hide through cliches. Questions are discouraged and giving answers is avoided. No one contradicts a position already taken. People avoid conflict and accountability by not talking to each other. Instead, they slide past each other. Discussion really means waiting for the boss to say what's right.

In one organization with which I am familiar this is carried to an extreme: At meetings, people who are supposed to give a report stand up and say their piece. Then the boss asks for comment. Someone always says "That was very interesting." Then the boss nods, thoughtfully, and thanks the first person for the report. Then the next person stands and delivers a report, which is always "interesting." Then that person is thanked. It's very common for people to repeat the last sentence or two of what was just said and nod their heads up and down, up and down, as though they were really thinking.

People in those kinds of organizations are like a long line of penguins. They're dressed for success. But while their feet point forward and they use words like *Initiate! Confront! Lead! Innovate!*, the truth is that they waddle from side to side. While their heads face forward, their eyes gaze skyward, toward those higher on the ladder. They're cautious and passive. Dependent and feeling vulnerable, they're endlessly looking for recognition, preoccupied with how they're doing.

Resentment and Ambivalence

In hierarchical organizations, there is basically very little real respect for people who are at the lower levels. Top-down, paternalistic organizations really do run in ways that express the belief that employees are not capable. Management tells subordinates the rules and subordinates learn them. The rules themselves say "I don't trust your judgment." Is it any wonder morale is poor?

Surveys in these organizations find employees very angry. They're saying "You don't show respect for us as individuals. You don't give me increasing responsibilities. You don't let me make decisions. You treat me like a child. You keep telling me what to do. You never ask me. You never listen to me. Besides that, you don't punish people who do nothing. I'm working my head off and you let those jerks get away with it. I end up having to do their work as well as my own. Why am I knocking myself out?"

But even as they resent being treated like children, being given rules to follow, people are also ambivalent. Rules give us an easy way to master situations. Rules gave us security and protect us from having to think and make judgments.

Dependence itself makes people ambivalent. Even though dependent people lean on the hierarchy to sustain and support them, they don't like being powerless. They want the support yet bitterly resent the fact that they need it. People resent the presumption of incompetence that underlies dependence. But without confidence, they remain dependent and more resentful than grateful.

This situation may partly explain why entitled people so often become greedy. In addition to grabbing for security, boxed into resenting what they get, they unconsciously also seek to get even by demanding even more.

Greed

In these organizations managers talk about what "I do for my people" and employees ask "What will you do for me?" Nowhere do we hear people say what they plan to do for themselves. Entitlement creates people who keep asking what else is going to be done for them. And what is done is never enough.

Arnold Jones, for example, spent most of his career with a large manufacturing company that has always taken pride in how it deals with its employees. He recently ran into Peter, a man from another division of the same company. They hadn't seen each other for a couple of years.

"What's happening?" Arnold asked.

"That damn company," Peter said. "First they force me to move from Stamford to Los Angeles. I hate Los Angeles, and so does my wife. I had to sell the house and pull the kids out of school. Then, less than a year later, they pull me back to Connecticut, for god's sake."

Peter happened to leave out one small detail: He'd gone to California as an executive in a division that lost $100 million during his tenure. He could have said, "We really screwed up. We lost a bundle. I'm really grateful I've still got a job. I'm going to give this one everything I've got." Instead, he said, "They jerked me around one more time. Damn them."

In 1989, a manager at IBM told me the company had just announced lower earnings, a buy-back of its stock, and a plan to cut costs by getting 10,000 people to take early retirement. In this belt-tightening atmosphere, an employee asked for an "open door," IBM's term for an employee complaint of unfair treatment; these complaints can be directed as high in the organization as the employee wants, all the way to the chairperson. "Imagine," this manager said, "this open door was brought by a guy with a high school education. He's a technician and he must be pretty good because he earns almost $90,000 a year. You know what he was complaining about? Getting a 6 percent raise! He said he was entitled to 11 percent because that's what he always got."

Another example of greed is illustrated by Sam Gershon, who went to work for a Fortune 500 company right out of college. He's serious and hard-working, always putting work first. No one salutes the corporate flag faster than he does.

But Sam's company hires the best. No matter how many hours he put in, he only made it to middle management. He's been plateaued at the same rank for about twelve years.

Profit margins have been under terrific pressure and the company's been downsizing for a few years. Sam's boss recently told him he was eligible for an early retirement package. Sam protested, "I don't want to retire. I'm only fifty-two. If I'm not here, where am I going to go? What am I going to do?"

Sam's boss said, "Sam, I can't tell you what to do. But I do know there's a chance your job is going to be eliminated. If you turn the retirement down, you'll have a job even if yours is cut. But I can't tell you what it will be or where it will be."

Sam is taking the package. He will get 60 percent of his salary and full health benefits for the rest of his life. Very indignantly, he told a friend, "Do you know what they just did? They cut my salary by 40 percent!"

What Entitlement Costs Us

The dollar cost of retirement packages to entitled employeese is only one reason we cannot afford to tolerate conditions of

Entitlement. The real cost to our nation is the loss of productivity, innovation, and creative thinking. Organizations will do better, will have more creative solutions to their issues, when they require performance. Morale is highest and people produce more and are most creative when there is pressure to perform.

Effect on Work Force

We psychologists have long been concerned with the debilitating effects of too much anxiety and we know that productivity suffers when uncertainty is high. But we've failed to realize the equally destructive effects of too little anxiety.

People are not at their keenest when life is too safe. When people receive without having to achieve they are protected from failure. There's no punishment for not achieving. At first glance that may seem like a good thing, but it is not. By protecting people from risk, we destroy their self-esteem. We rob them of the opportunity to become strong, competent people.

Facing risk is the only way we gain confidence, because confidence is the result of mastering challenge. Confidence is an internal state. It cannot be given; it can only be earned. The only way to get genuinely confident is to be familiar with fear and then conquer it. In order to learn we must also occasionally fail. We get courage, the strength to do something new, only when we have learned to see a failure as a battle and not the war. Without courage, no one takes risks; without taking risks, no one develops courage.

Thus, too little anxiety is destructive. It deprives people of the experiences that create confidence. They never learn how to push past risk to success. They never have the opportunity to develop skills of coping, of somehow managing to pull it off even when being unsure.

Instead of strength, courage, and confidence, people trapped by Entitlement are cautious and avoid risk. When security is very high and people shouldn't be afraid, they are. Entitled people cling to Entitlement, fearing they couldn't earn or compete or survive on their own. The long-term result of too much protection is an endless search for protection because you're afraid of losing it.

In the short run, requiring that people earn what they receive is vastly harsher than simply giving it to them. But in the long run, it is the only way that people can gain self-esteem and independence.

Effect on Productivity

If all this seems a bit too psychological, let me put it in very concrete, bottom-line terms: When people are not held accountable for performance levels, they don't perform. Instead, they become complacent ("I've got it made") or apathetic ("If it doesn't matter one way or the other, why try? Who cares?").

What happens to involvement and motivation if we have a nation of people saying "Who cares?" What happens to productivity?

Productivity is always low whenever there is Entitlement.

We must shake loose the psychology of Entitlement. We must empower people by giving them responsibilities and we must hold them accountable for their actions. Only in this way can we engender the achievement, growth, and confidence that are necessary for maximum productivity.

Breaking the Cycle

Quite simply, American business and industry can no longer afford to sustain Entitlement. We cannot continue to carry underproductive people. Today, as the rate of change grows continuously faster, we need people who are confident enough to cope with tomorrow's unpredictable problems. People who have been entitled find themselves without the skills they need to cope with changes. They don't have the discipline to persevere, the confidence to withstand uncertainty, or the courage to initiate and innovate. We have reached a critical junction.

Uprooting Entitlement is not easy. It's hard to get people to give up the warm blanket of protection. People who have been accustomed to years of Entitlement will resist increments of risk. They will resist accountability and flee from evaluations. People naturally gravitate to the setting where they feel most comfortable or secure, and they will fight any change from that. That's why Entitlement is so hard to uproot.

To make things even tougher, wherever Entitlement exists it is usually codified in the organization's rules and enshrined in its culture. Thus, it often takes a significant shock to the system, the motivation of crisis, to change things. Since moving away from Entitlement by definition requires risk taking, it will always involve fear. That is the subject of the next chapter.

3

When Organizations Are Too Stressed—The Paralysis of Fear

George Beeler knows about fear. A skilled tool and die maker who has worked in the automobile industry for thirty years, he remembers "when Detroit defined the physical laws of the auto universe." Today, however, the competitive pressure is so bad that "no union could help him now."*

George works for a supplier to Ford. Ford is currently trying to develop more Japanese-style supplier relationships: long-term partnerships with fewer suppliers. In endless dread, Beeler constantly rehearses the scene when an irritatingly young inspector from Ford is going to stand in the middle of the shop floor and announce that since his company failed Ford's quality

---

*George Beeler is in a very different position from the UAW members who work directly for the Big Three auto companies. The UAW insists on industrywide contracts. In 1993, the UAW first established the contract with Ford and then imposed agreement on GM. General Motors lost $17 billion in the United States in the 1990s.

Nonetheless, the UAW insisted that GM agree to continue a job and income protection plan that was first agreed to in 1990. Workers are given up to 95 percent of their full pay when they're laid off, even for jobs that were eliminated back in 1987. In June of 1994, GM was offering idled UAW members as much as $60,000 to move to four points where there was a need for them. Employees who accept the offer receive $25,000 as a "signing bonus" and will receive additional bonuses after the first and second year they've been in the new job.

test, it is being dropped. If Ford drops this supplier, George's employer will close down. He says:

> I don't know what will happen. I'm just fighting for my life. I'm not scared of changing. I just want the opportunity to survive. I'm a tiny part of a big machine and I can't tell who's running things. Detroit? Washington? Tokyo? We're all under the ax right now. You drop that ax on these companies, and you're dropping the ax on a whole damn world. That's the world of my father and my son. That's my world.

An employee of a large utility company knows about fear:

> I'd feel more happy in my job if I knew I wasn't going to get laid off. . . . I could work better . . . now I have stomachaches all the time 'cause I'm always wondering. I'm not kidding. I have an ulcer wondering what's going to happen. In the past there was a lot of satisfaction knowing there was job security and you could perform with no risk. Now you could lose your job even if you do hustle. My supervisor asked me if I'd like to become a supervisor. You got to be kidding. That's like cutting off your own throat . . . because those are the guys they're laying off. When you're out there working, you need your mind on what you're doing, and not worrying about "Are you going to lose your job tomorrow?"

Layoffs, or the specter of layoffs, are a very real source of fear. And there is no end in sight. For four years in a row (1987–1990), according to surveys by the American Management Association, roughly a third of American companies cut their payrolls. In late 1990, journalist Ron Zemke noted that the estimates of how many managers have been cut since the 1981–1982 recession vary from 1.5 to 3 million. The search for increased efficiency, higher productivity, and lower costs continues.* While the largest cuts are being made in corporations, governments, quasi-governmental organizations like the post office, hospitals, universities, and nonprofit associations and foundations are also downsizing. Cutting jobs is not restricted to the United States. While the cuts are much smaller than the United States has experienced, downsizing is also happening in Canada, England, Scotland, Russia, and even Japan. Zemke reports that even among lifetime employers like Sony, Mitsubishi, Honda, and Toyota, there are tentative moves to cut the ranks of professionals and managers. Japanese basic industries, like steel, have gone through severe restructurings in order to maintain profits and markets.

What Fear Is Like

Layoffs, hostile takeovers, and massive corporate restructuring are tangible. The fear they create is easy to see. People talk about fear of losing their jobs, or frustration that promotion opportunities have diminished, or resentment as they're asked to contribute more to their health insurance. While those are certainly real issues, they are also the specific expression of a generalized anxiety that can paralyze people and companies.†

*John A. Byrne, "The Pain of Downsizing," *Business Week*, May 9, 1994, pp. 60–69. Byrne reports the following cuts in staff since early 1991: IBM (85,000); AT&T (83,500); GM (74,000); U.S. Postal Service (55,000); Sears (50,000); Boeing (30,000); NYNEX (22,000). Hughes Aircraft (21,000); GTE (17,000); Martin Marietta (15,000); Dupont (14,800); Eastman Kodak (14,000); Philip Morris (14,000); Procter & Gamble (13,000); Phar Mor (13,000); Bank of America (12,000); Aetna (11,800); GE Aircraft Engines (10,250); McDonnell Douglas (10,200); BellSouth (10,200); Ford Motor Co. (10,000); Xerox (10,000); Pacific Telesis (10,000); Honeywell (9,000); U.S. West (9,000).

†In this book I usually use the term Fear1 for this paralyzing anxiety because we all understand what the word means. From a psychological standpoint, anxiety is different from fear. Fears are specific: "I'm afraid to lose my job because a new one might mean moving." Anxiety, in contrast, is generalized: "When I think about losing my job I get sick to my stomach, because without that, there's nothing to hang on to." Fears are concrete; anxiety is pervasive. Anxiety is a whole lot worse than fear. Fears can be transformed into specific issues to be dealt with. Anxiety is the amorphous feeling that something is terribly wrong, and it is this anxiety that we see in many restructuring organizations.

When people are frozen, waiting for the ax to fall, they don't get much work done.

The crux of excessive anxiety is the feeling that you have no control over what is happening to you. You cannot even influence what's happening. At work, it's as though the playing field is no longer level. You no longer have a manageable deal. You've lost the sense that if you do your part, you can make it okay. You've lost the feeling that you know the rules. Anxiety makes people feel like victims.

Fear in Our Organizations

When anxiety is high, cynicism rises and morale sinks. Inevitably that has a powerful effect on people's dedication to the organization. Companies will not get gung-ho performance from people who are scared, cynical, resentful, apathetic, and mistrustful.

In a study conducted in 1989 and repeated in 1990, the Philadelphia outplacement firm Right Associates reported that human resources executives in 500 companies cited aftershocks from downsizing that profoundly affected everyone involved. They saw low morale in surviving employees, fear of future cuts, and mistrust of management (74 percent in 1989, 80 percent in 1990). Middle managers appear more stressed, seem tired all the time, are stretched thin, and seem to be close to burnout. They act as thought they have less control over what's going on around them.

In another poll conducted by Right Associates, 74 percent of senior managers at recently downsized companies said that their workers had low morale, feared future cutbacks, and distrusted management. Consultant Gary Neilson of Booz Allen & Hamilton in Chicago said, "The whole quality of decision-making suffers. Employees are always looking over their shoulders. Managers are afraid to take risks."

Fear Smothers Productivity

The significant point for U.S. business is, of course, that downsizing has a direct, bottom-line relationship to productivity. During the height of the layoffs at GE, when people expected productivity to soar, productivity crept along at a disheartening rate of 2.5 percent annually. Some companies have tried to estimate the cost of doom and gloom. In 1987, Bell & Howell was in a three-way takeover skirmish for half the year and rumors of layoffs were everywhere. Everyone felt too depleted and dispirited to work much. Bell & Howell executives have estimated that the drop in productivity for that half year may have cut profits by 11 percent, or $2.1 million.

Writing in *Fortune*, Ronald Henkoff says:

> Administered in repeated doses, [downsizing] can hurt product quality, alienate customers, and actually cut productivity growth. It can foster an organization so preoccupied with bean counting, so anxious about where the ax will fall next, that employees become narrow-minded, self-absorbed, and risk-averse. . . . More than half the 1,468 restructured companies surveyed by the Society for Human Resource Management reported that employee productivity either stayed the same or deteriorated after the layoffs.

The Changing Contract

While most employees fully understand the reason for the changes in the old employment contract that promised almost complete job security, still for many these changes feel like a betrayal of trust. Especially for those facing a loss of security or jobs, the changes are experienced emotionally as a breaking of faith. When you can no longer count on the institution that was your emotional center, what can you count on?*

---

*NYNEX is another good example. In 1971 New York Telephone had 103,000 employees. In May 1994, it was down to 40,220 and announced it would further reduce the payroll by 15,000 to 25,000 people. Not surprisingly, morale kept spinning lower and lower. There was emotional trauma for everyone involved: for the executives who ordered the cuts and selected those who left, for those laid off and their families, and for the survivors who got to keep their jobs but often in a very changed organization in which trust levels had been assaulted. Robert Thrasher is the executive in charge of NYNEX's downsizing. He's been called the "corporate assassin," and "Thrasher

The new contract is well illustrated by what happened at
AT&T. Before the divestiture in 1984, the giant phone company was a stable organization that offered lifetime employment. The company imposed universal standards that permitted no deviance and created standards of service that required
shelves of rule books.

Now AT&T operates in a wholly competitive environment
and the competition is global, not just domestic. It's had two
major layoffs, early retirement, acquisitions, sales, and mergers.
Now it is competing for customers. When you're trying to keep
customers, your people have to be flexible. They can't be continuously thumbing through the rule books.

The old AT&T gave people immense psychological security because they were told exactly what to do in every imagin-
able circumstance. The new AT&T is now telling people to do
the reverse. From a risk aversive culture where mistakes were
punished, AT&T is trying to become a gutsy place that rewards
innovation and decisiveness. No wonder long-term employees
are feeling uncomfortable.

"The old company cared," they say. "The new company
doesn't. Now, when I can't be sure my job is safe, how do I know
I can trust you?"

It is the beginning of the psychology of Fear: The old rules
are gone and the new rules don't make sense.

What Panicked People Do

The essence of Fear, remember, is the sense that you have no
control over what's happening to you. When people feel pow-

---

the Slasher." He disconnected his home answering machine because the tape
was filled with obscenities and threats. A middle manager who's a 20-year
veteran of NYNEX said, "The officers all have golden parachutes. They're in
charge of their own fates. We're not involved. We're just affected. Even if people won't be fired this time, they're still frightened of the future. It affects
their self-esteem and their pocketbook. And most people aren't going from
something to something. They have no place to go."

In the short term there is no doubt that downsizing impacts morale negatively. But the long-term outcome is less certain. The outcome could be
largely positive when paired with a reduction in bureaucracy. Other possible
gains include improved quality and customer service and a greater willingness
among surviving employees to take risks.

erless, they are preoccupied with issues of power because they never feel safe. Their antennae are constantly sweeping the air, testing for other people's intentions. They're forever scanning for subtle cues of coercion, of malevolence, of territorial incursion, of exertions to control them. Psychologically battered, they often become:

Narcissistic:	"I'm watching out for number one."
Paranoid:	"I think everyone's out to get me."
Territorial:	"I'm grabbing my turf and surrounding it with barbed wire."
Rigid:	"I'm hanging on to what I know."
Cynical:	"I'll believe it when I see it."
Political:	"I'm keeping my eyes open."

Denial

Facing enormous, life-shattering changes, the first thing many people do is deny that anything has changed, that anything is wrong. When Fear has replaced Entitlement, people try to re-create their sense of being in control and being secure.

Resistance to change is normal behavior, because change is inherently stressful. In Fear, there's so much stress that people can resist even acknowledging it.

Worry

Whenever people or organizations are in Fear, they will be hypersensitive to the possibility that there's more bad news. Fear generates fear. Thus, when anxiety increases, so do rumors. No one knows what's happening. People make up worst-case scenarios. They're nervous and jerky. They look for commiseration. They complain on the phone and they mythologize the past when everything was great. Sometimes management tries to sustain employee morale by denying that anything is wrong, in turn creating a vacuum that becomes filled with rumors.

A former CBS employee described what things were like at the height of the network's cost cutting:

There were a couple of months where we sat around
and worried all day. Then we started to worry that we
were worrying too much, so we went back to work for
ten minutes. Then somebody would call up and say,
"Did you see the papers this morning? Are you getting laid off?" So we'd go back to worrying again.

Worried people don't get a lot of work done. Most of their
psychological energy is taken up in trying to manage how they
feel. When they're worried about themselves, they don't worry
about the organization and how it's doing. They're more likely
to spend a lot of time in the corridors, at the water cooler, in
the cafeteria, or in each other's offices. And they're very likely
to put on black expressions and shut up when the boss is pass-
ing by.

Inconsistent Behavior Patterns

When people are in Fear, their behavior is often extreme
and frequently inconsistent. Sometimes they'll acknowledge
their issues and often they won't. People will alternate working
harder to try to get things under control with giving up, accepting fate, or denying anything is wrong. As people get closer to
burnout, which is the sense of not having *any* control over what
happens to them, they often become more passive and less decisive.

In Fear, people can take on too many risks either out of
desperation to change the situation or because they feel that
things are so bad they can't get much worse. Or people may
rigidly and compulsively follow the rules with a ferocious energy that drains them, because unconsciously they are trying to
create order out of chaos.

Coping Techniques

Good Behavior

When reality forces people to acknowledge that security is
gone, they try to wrest some sense of control from an amor-

phous universe. Often they do that by being "good." That's why they bite into the rules, clutch the regulations, and repeat things they already know, things they've already mastered.

When people are scared they keep their eyes on the people in power. The ratio of "yes people" rises exponentially. Until people are able to leave the situation, they will try to keep in good graces, so they placate and please those with power. They will try to avoid conflict and disagreement. They will focus on politics, on pleasing their superiors, and they'll avoid the differences in opinion that are the substance of real work.

Self-Protection

Fear often makes people grab on to territory so they have something to control and defend. Everyone else is a potential predator because they're out to protect themselves also, so no one can be trusted. Hal Burlingame, senior vice-president for Human Resources of AT&T, described the effects of divestiture and especially the trauma of downsizing:

> While major corporate upheavals have tended to draw people in other businesses more closely together, circling the wagons, our upheaval has caused the walls between units to become higher and stronger. Rather than drawing together, our people have narrowed their focus and strengthened their allegiance to their own entity, their own department, or their own work unit.

In Fear, there's no real ambition because there's no energy left. Energy is used for hanging on.

After Pacific Gas and Electric downsized, reorganized, and lost its monopoly because of deregulation, anxiety soared. The result, according to more than half of the employees, was a decline in people working together in order to assure the company's interest. Instead, people set out to protect their turf. "We seem to change direction daily, not through creativity and innovation, but through personal power struggles and inefficiency. One of the most significant obstacles facing PG&E

employees today is continuing turf battles which hinder communication and cooperation among departments."

When people are scared and clinging to safety there's no commitment to the whole. You don't get teamwork. As a result, organizational citizenship drops out. People stop helping others, they don't put in more time than is strictly required, and they won't share information.

Unrelenting competition causes the same territorial behavior. People won't cooperate with others and they won't communicate, because helping others improve their performance can jeopardize one's own competitive success. That's the way it's been at GM because the way up the ladder has historically been to outperform colleagues. When Roger Smith was chairman, he said that territorial pride often outweighed the corporate good. "There's some guy out there in an accounts-payable department, looking over that sea of heads bowed down over their little stamps and saying, 'It's mine, all mine.' "

Seeking Safety

When there's a significant increase in uncertainty, there's always a tendency to go back to styles of coping that used to provide comfort.

Some people will try to flee the situation either by actually leaving or through denial, which takes them mentally away from a reality that's overwhelming. Some people become rigid and refuse to do anything they haven't done many times before. GM's Roger Smith has called these people the "frozen middle management." Some people get so scared they don't do anything at all.

When anxiety is very high, some people try to be invisible. They're afraid to be noticed, so they conform even more than before. They're afraid to be visible because the rules aren't clear anymore and they could be seen as deviates, mavericks, or trouble makers.

Scared, because it's no longer possible to know how to get secure, people try to make sure they're not making mistakes. When anxiety is very high, the natural tendency will be for decisions to be pushed higher and higher up the ladder. When anxiety is very high and people want to avoid risks of any kind, they will delegate decisions upward.

Delegating upward, asking for permission, is a way to avoid risk. A good example took place in one of the regional Bells. The Bells, as we all know, are trying to shake up the too-secure culture they inherited from AT&T. Their people know the right words to say, but it's hard to shake off the cautions of Entitlement.

Managers in this particular Bell wanted to encourage the delegation of decision-making downward, so they eliminated an entire level of management. There had been five levels and now there were four. The result was that fewer and fewer decisions got made. After level four was eradicated, everyone who was at level three went up to level five to get permission to do things. There were't enough people at level five to go around.

When anxiety is very high, decision making will increasingly be a function of committees. The result will be committees that never confront issues or each other. Many decisions will not be made and those that are will be compromises.

Solace in the Hierarchy

In Fear, people look for support from authority. They seek solace in the hierarchy. A hierarchy serves many functions. Besides the obvious ones like defining responsibility, increasing coordination, and assigning decision making, it helps people deal with anxiety. Hierarchies comfort because they tell people where they belong and what they are supposed to do. They provide approval and acceptance from those with greater authority. When anxiety is very high, people need reassurance the most. Then people are desperate for the assurance from authority that things will be better.

Fear in Action

Now let us see how these psychological truths play out in the real world. The three companies discussed here are real, and their industries and the data given are real; the only omissions are real names.

Energy Company—The Vicious Cycle of Fear

In the early 1980s, one of our largest energy companies was filled with enormous enthusiasm. It had a mission: Through its energy programs it would save the nation!

The corporation had always hired the very best graduates from the very best universities. And the implicit contract was, "Because you're one of the best, and we're going to ask you for some sacrifices, if you work reasonably hard, you'll have an exciting career with positions of responsibility and you'll be paid well. We welcome you on board and expect you'll be with us for a long time. Most of our people stay with us for the whole of their career."

Then, in May 1986, the price of oil plummeted and the corporation announced plans to slash the work force. A "voluntary" retirement program was instituted, budgets were cut, projects were eliminated, and parts of the company were sold or relocated. Although very few people were actually fired, people's perception of their security changed as the company moved from Entitlement to Fear.

Even though it was generally understood why the cutbacks and reorganization were necessary, many still felt betrayed and angry. Since people tend to trust their own managers with whom they've worked, a lot of blame and mistrust were directed at top management.

Employees entered the vicious cycle of fear. They strategized for their survival by doing only what they were told, taking no risks, and second-guessing everything. As anxiety rose, so did dependence. Their increased need for support from the leadership they did not trust eroded their self-esteem and taught them they were victims. Learned helplessness increased their dependence and victimization. And the cycle continued.

After the reorganization, the corporation's leadership analyzed the reaction of the organization as a whole to the heightened stress. They called it psychic gridlock.

When people stopped trusting the company, they tried to protect their territory by competing for resources, which had several effects. Conflict over resources led to an increase in office politics. Instead of focusing on the needs of the organization, people concentrated on getting what they could get for themselves.

Competition for resources also resulted in a loss of reserves. Combined with the increased office politics, the emphasis was on the short term. The organization as a whole got cautious. No one took risks. People distorted information in order to protect themselves.

Since reserves were down, there was no cushion. Everything became an emergency, so management increased its controls. Power became increasingly centralized, but since caution dominated, there was no horizontal communication and all vertical communication was top-down. The top of the pyramid was ignorant of what was going on below it.

As resources got tighter, management moved to eliminate what it called nonessentials. Some of those were largely symbolic, like personalized notepads. In the face of all the takeaways, morale plummeted and the executives exerted more and more control. The amount of required paperwork grew enormously. With a sort of gallows humor, people talked about having to measure and record "how long the pencils are." Because the situation was not contained, controls increased. There were more surveillance procedures, more rules, and more time spent enforcing rules.

That's when gridlock moved into the full-blown overcontrol syndrome. There was a big increase in pressure to "do what you're told; this is the way we do things." As a result, conformity increased, risk taking declined, communication decreased, rumors increased, and trust, efficiency, and adaptation decreased. The defense—the attempt to cope with anxiety—had become a part of the problem.

Communications Company—The Impact of Unremitting Anxiety

This high-tech communications company was a pioneer in its field. There was a vast and growing market for its products and technology. Belong long the company was bought by a much larger, more traditional communications company. The marriage between the original free spirits and the more straitlaced managers of the buyer created enormous anxiety. Then, international competition exploded, diminishing the company's market share. Worse, the core business is now mature and is no longer fast-growing and entrepreneurial. In the start-up days of the company, anxiety could trigger very positive energies. Now anxiety can generate only more anxiety.

Within the company, no critical, final decisions are being made. In fact, none have been made for a long time. Many of the company's original employees have left for other organizations where the future seems surer and there's some sense of control. In the face of anxiety and depression, the surviving employees are laying a lot of blame on the new owner. Whether the company were bought or not, its spirit would no longer be exuberant because it doesn't own the market anymore. But it's not emotionally satisfying to say "Economic conditions have changed!" It's vastly more sustaining to have a living target to blame for trouble.

In this company, sustained depression and prolonged anxiety have resulted in the loss of any sense of membership in a team or being part of an organization. The high levels of anxiety have increased employee preoccupation with what's going to happen to them. Self-absorbed, each individual is separate from everyone else. People feel alone and very vulnerable. While employees are asking the new owner for support and compassion, the buyer is saying "Enough! Move forward. Go!"

Utility Company—Confusion of a New Environment

Before deregulation of the industry, this company had a monopoly on supplying energy to its territory. The monopoly is now gone and the company must find its way through the strange environment of a competitive marketplace.

Employees have remained loyal to this company in the wake of major changes and they want to help make the company successful against the competition, but they are in conflict. They hear the words *market-driven* and they aren't sure how they will be affected. They're feeling anxious because they haven't figured out how to combine the spirit of public service with cost efficiency. They realize the market has become competitive and they need to take moderate risks, but they don't know how. More than anything, they're afraid they're going to lose the soul of their organization. In the midst of the transitions that generate anxiety, they're not sure of the direction management is taking and they're not confident that management knows where it's going.

In the wake of change, the level of trust has declined. The majority of people in the bargaining unit don't feel they're in a trusting work environment, nor does half of middle management, nor do one-third of the executives. The feeling that senior management doesn't trust middle management permeates the organization.

A lack of trust in specifics soon becomes a lack of trust in everything—it becomes generalized. For example, many employees don't trust the credibility of internal corporate publications on sensitive or controversial issues. They think top-down communication can't be trusted. Many are convinced the grapevine is the best source of information on what's happening. And they're cynical about upward communication, because they're convinced no one is listening. Cynicism also becomes generalized: "Management wants us to think they really care about our opinions. But that's only what they want us to think. They're not going to do anything with what we say."

Researchers at the utility company found there were dramatic changes in how employees perceived the company. People were asked to think about the old and the new companies as though they were people and then to describe them in terms of personality qualities. People felt the market-driven strategy changed the organization fundamentally. The words used to describe the old organization were warm and emotional: *family-oriented, caring, loyal, honest, competent,* and *confident.* While they said it was too bureaucratic, they also said it had been a fun, social, family-oriented organization that valued older, experienced people. Now, the rising stars were younger, educated, white-collar yuppies straight out of school. That's why, they said, there's been a decline in competence.

Employees described the new organization as schizophrenic. It has the contradictory qualities of being both authoritarian and entrepreneurial, cautious and innovative. It has kept all the bad qualities of the "old" organization and has lost everything that was positive. It's still bureaucratic, but without any warmth.

They also described the new organization as insecure and chaotic. It's a place of stress, fear, selfishness, and short-sightedness. Most important, employees feel the company has lost its integrity and competence.

Almost half of the employees in this company feel their work is not appreciated and less than a third say they get positive feedback when they do good work. Only 18 percent think good work is rewarded. The great majority, 74 percent, are skeptical that doing a good job will make their future any more secure. Among employees at all levels morale is at an all-time low.

Lessons to Learn

What the Boss Has to Do

In conditions of Fear, there is no trust. In organizations undergoing the turbulence of major change, when employees are least able to trust, that's just when they are being asked to trust their leaders to get them through the period of anxiety.

In such a situation, whoever has more power needs to understand the dysfunctional consequences of feeling that things are out of control. Thus, those in charge shouldn't add to the anxiety.

Some managers and executives try to gain control by becoming tough. Sometimes being tough is the leadership the situation requires. Toughness can be constructive. However, when an organization or an individual is already very anxious, unrelenting and capricious demands will increase the anxiety level.

Peter Nulty found that being tough can be constructive, but it's a high-risk style because "the boss constantly plays chicken with the limits of his subordinate's endurance."

Since there's tremendous resistance to giving up Entitlement, and there will be a continual drift back to the security of Entitlement whenever pressure is lessened, change will require consistent and constructive toughness when it comes to requiring performance and resisting dependence. But when anxiety is already high and the need is to move from Fear, the most effective style will use reasonable, predictable, and articulated psychological support, conveying, especially, the ways in which security can be earned.

The Positive Side of Anxiety

The 1980s were a time of crisis. Many of our institutions needed to change and many more still do. In effect, they have to pay for the accumulated inefficiencies that Entitlement permitted. In a market economy, old structures and techniques are destroyed and replaced when they no longer function well. Though the process is often painful, the result is a dynamic renewal.

This period of turbulence, then, is an awful ending of some certainties and assumptions. There is the end of job security for people at all levels, the end of certainty about the future, and the early end of promotion for many. Those ends must be accepted as ends and must be converted to beginnings. Those ends are the opportunities for organizations to get lean and to push power down.

As long as it is not so high as to be disabling, Fear is the great motivator. While it is true that the restructuring and the downsizing are causing serious pain, they are also resulting in organizations that are in much better shape to operate in the continuous turbulence of a world economy in the 1990s.

The psychology of Fear can lead to the psychology of Earning, which is the upside of Fear. Once we have a clear vision of what we are doing, we can guide our organizations toward Earning by leading them deliberately but compassionately out of Entitlement through the necessary step of Fear.

Finding just the right level of Fear and managing it is vastly different from watching helplessly as companies flounder under the effects of Fear that come from external economic difficulties. Deliberately, strategically moving organizations from Entitlement to Earning, by way of optimal levels of Fear, is described in later chapters. Probably the greatest of the dangers is the loss of all sense of Fear, because then we will inevitably slide back to the disabling comfort of Entitlement.

4

When Organizations Are Revitalized — The Energy of Earning

In a nondescript building in a commercial section of San Diego, there is a vision of the future, a merger of the baby-boomer ideals of fun and sharing with a tough-minded drive to succeed financially. Industrial Computer Source was formed by a group of people disillusioned with their former employer, a major computer company with a classic Silicon Valley culture.

The company they left is famous. Everyone wears jeans and leaves at 4 P.M. on Friday for beer. There was supposed to be profit sharing, with employees owning a large portion of the company's stock. The company's president was recently quoted as saying "Working here is like being self-employed."

Although this situation sounds ideal, the vice-president for finance at the new company says, "We worked like dogs in crummy conditions. Supposedly we were all sacrificing for the good of all, but all we were really doing was making the president richer. We made the profits and he got to keep them."

The motto of the old company is "Make do and do without." That would have been fine if there had been a payoff in sight, but there was none.

In six years, the new company has gone from zero to $15 million in sales and has no debt. In 1988, thirty-one people earned a total of $1.3 million. Pretax profit in 1990 was $2.4

million. At the end of every shipping day the profits for the day are posted.

One of the founders says:

> The profit is handed down right away and it's not in stock options. Everyone knows how much money we've made. At the end of the quarter, everyone gets a piece of it. Immediately. We never had a quarter with a loss. Hourly people get a month's pay and the rest of us get 10 percent.
>
> Not only that, we pay 110 percent of the top price for salaries for all positions. So even if the owner— and there is one guy who owns most of it—even if he didn't give you a bonus, you'd still have made more money than you could have anywhere else. We expect everyone to work like hell. That's part of the deal and everybody knows it.
>
> We got terrific people here and they're here because they want to be part of the next phase because we're growing so fast. If we grow, we're geniuses. If we don't, we'll be in trouble with the special people we hired. But we tell the truth and everyone knows what's happening, so I think we'll be okay.
>
> There's a difference between financial and psychological quality. In the other company, they talked both and delivered on neither. We're trying to do both, but especially financial. The psychological stuff just happens. At the end of the day I'm physically tired because I worked for ten hours. But I'm not emotionally tired. Our success is tangible so we feel competent and optimistic.
>
> We've got a pleasant environment and nice people. Ultimately the president says "go/no go" or "spend/don't spend," but for the most part we all do whatever we have to. Everybody does whatever is necessary.
>
> When we moved into this building, everybody got in and cleaned and painted. The president too. We had vice-presidents making shelves along with assem-

blers. We didn't want the niggardly mentality of the other company here so we got nice space.

I found the new space notable for its nondescriptness. In front, there are some ordinary parking spaces; none are reserved. Inside, there's little physical evidence of status. It's a reflection of the relative unimportance of hierarchy.

Of course, there is a hierarchy. There's a president who put up most of the money; he owns more of the company than anyone else. Some officers who were founders have a significant share. There are many others who have no shares. In terms of how everyone works, hierarchical power is pretty unnecessary. In practice, most of the time, no one works for someone else. People don't ask what their job is; they find out what needs to be done. In general terms, they are told what they're supposed to accomplish. Then they go and do it. More than anything, there's a camaraderie in the pursuit of more success.

Competition is a terrific motivator in the new company. It has gained a lot of energy from its desire to prove something to the old company. Because employees felt betrayed, this competition is partly fueled by vengeance. The synergy of successful growth and successful vengeance is powerful.

As an organization the company is winning because it's getting bigger faster than the old company. Within a few years at this rate of growth, it will overtake the old company. When it's bigger than the old company, it's going to take on the industry leader. War is fun when you're winning.

Everyone who works at Industrial Computer Source feels like a winner. The products stand ready to be shipped, right near the offices. The offices are off a corridor near the assembly room. The lunch room is right in the middle. It's bright and clean inside, lit by the southern California sun. Posted on the wall for everyone to see are yesterday's numbers.

The Essence of Earning

What we are seeing in Industrial Computer Source is an organization experiencing the natural high of success, of Earning.

The climate of Earning is purposeful, disciplined energy. In start-up companies like Industrial Computer Source, the environment itself provides the stimulus. In more mature organizations, enlightened leaders will have to engineer the conditions that create Earning.

At Earning environment requires realistic opportunities to achieve and realistic requirements to do so. It requires parameters of achievement so there's pressure to perform and some certainty when you have performed. It requires accurate matching of requirements to ability so that you're right more often than you're wrong.

People with a psychology of Earning know they're winners, but they also know they're always being judged. Although past achievements get you into today's game, only today's achievements will get you into tomorrow's game. Earning is the end result of a continuous tension in which people are under pressure to perform, but they have the means to reduce the pressure through achievement.

And they are not afraid. To people with a mind-set of Earning, that medium level of pressure makes things exciting. They have learned that change is an opportunity to experience challenge, and that mastering challenge is the only way to *earn* the experience of being right, of being first, of being a winner.

Thus, a psychology of earning is a psychology of winning. People discover that when they accept risk, they benefit. They develop techniques to cope with the stress, and uncertainty is not as frightening to them. They will face increased challenge by attempting to achieve more.

The attitude of Earning recognizes this basic fact of human psychology: People prefer accountability; they want to be rewarded when they work hard and they want those who don't to be punished. They want their work to be judged because it is the only way to feel that their work is significant. People with a psychology of Earning will tend not to respect people who don't earn their success. For them, trying is not enough; accomplishment will be a requirement for respect.

Therefore, this attitude requires that people begin with some level of self-confidence and are willing to work to acquire more. Being willing to be judged takes courage and it takes confidence.

The only people able to move beyond the psychologies of Entitlement or Fear are those who have achieved enough to feel confident. Confidence is empowering. Empowered, people feel able to take on more risks. They become better able to earn and accept responsibility and autonomy. They feel that they're heard, they're involved, they're effective, they make decisions, and they make a difference. Taking on risk, working, and then succeeding creates more of a sense of empowerment. It's a wonderful, energizing cycle of positive accomplishments.

Practice Benefits

Organizations that have or create an Earning environment reap increased productivity, increased innovation, and increased teamwork. It's not hard to see that an energized work force contributes directly to the bottom line.

Productivity

Americans traditionally believed that all people should earn their own way. That was a moral judgment, but we didn't realize that it was also an enabling point of view. Being held to task is the only way people can develop confidence and independence. It's also the only condition under which larger systems can be productive.

The equivalent of productivity in an organization is problem solving by an individual. In both cases, the result is confidence and thus courage. That's why we say that the psychology of Earning is the real secret of productivity. Only where there's a psychology of Earning do people achieve, solve problems, more forward, change, and adapt. Problems are not solved and anxiety is not reduced by hugging trees or bureaucratic security blankets. With an attitude of Earning you articulate the problem, address it directly, and solve it incrementally.

Innovation

In these days of make-or-break competition, it is particularly worth noting the connection between Earning and innovation. Earning and empowerment are preconditions for creativity, especially when big breakthroughs are involved. Creativity involves what psychologists call "breaking set," seeing things differently from how they've been seen before. Breaking set involves taking a risk because being different is usually perceived initially as being wrong.

Confidence is the critical ingredient in being able to leave the security of what's known and familiar and move into the new and unfamiliar. Only people who have earned confidence will be able to stop clinging to precedent and relying on rules. Confidence earned through the experience of achieving is a prerequisite for being able to disagree, especially with those people who have greater power. Only when people feel respected for what they've achieved can they give up the safety of being "yes people."

In Earning organizations there may be rules, but it's understood that rules may be broken because circumstances are always changing. People are encouraged to ask "Do we do what we did before, or do we try something new? Do we follow precedent or do we have to tend or ignore the rule?" This kind of questioning frees people from confinement, so they are psychologically able to deviate from what occurred before and they are therefore better able to be creative or innovative.

Teamwork

In this kind of environment, teamwork flourishes. The effective team is made up of individuals who are confident in their talent. While individuals are capable of being innovators, their esteem makes it possible for them to work collaboratively, disciplined under someone's leadership for the good of the whole. Teams are most successful when the members are entrepreneurs but are willing to harness their ability to the unit's purposes and capabilities.

Respect for the other person's contribution is the real basis of teamwork. It isn't the result of a particular method of operating but rather the result of a fundamental attitude: "Other people know something I'll benefit from hearing." Teamwork is the expression of a willingness to collaborate because you respect the others. All those involved in making decisions have earned that right and are comfortable with the responsibility and the power. They're also comfortable because they're very confident in their ability.

You can't have a team psychology when people are preoccupied with protecting themselves. Management exhortations or training for team skills are nonproductive in Entitlement or Fear because in both cases people are too insecure to be able to contribute to the well-being of others. They can't risk the possibility that others might end up looking better.

Where there is a psychology of Earning, people feel they're part of a community. Because they don't feel the need to gain more power to protect themselves, people are able to hear others. When you can hear, you're better able to appreciate the needs of and work to the betterment of the team or the organization as a whole. Team members are competitive in the sense that no one wants to look bad in front of the people they respect. Everyone's opinion is on the table where it will be judged by everyone else. There's electricity in the air because opinions are always being evaluated and challenged. Because people are not defensive, no one needs to win at the expense of the others.

Thus, people in empowered teams are colleagues at the same time they are competitors. It's what I call creative tension—that mixture of cooperation and competition that leads to attempts at improvement, to the end of complacency, to the drive to innovation and ever-better decisions.

This blend of competition and cooperation is probably optimal in raising effort and productivity to their highest levels. As people find their team creates more excitement and far better performance than they had as individuals, it becomes easier to contribute selflessly to the team. Team commitment is also greater when individuals have the opportunity to feel that they are successful in the team and that the team is a successful competitor.

Motivation for Excellence

When we think about what we need to do to create and sustain high levels of morale in organizations, we never think of hard work and pressure to produce. And yet, where would you expect morale to be higher? In a rich organization where carpets are deep and walls are paneled and there's all the time in the world to investigate and discuss and write reports, or in a brand-new entrepreneurial organization where people are putting in sixteen-hour days and the whole thing will sink or swim depending on the quality and speed with which they can produce a new idea and get the product out?

The best morale builder, the greatest motivator, is success, that is, earning the status of being a winner.

To create the climate where this attitude can thrive, we must understand what drives people to Earning behaviors. What motivates good work? What provides a sense of enrichment and fulfillment?

In the past twelve years I have given hundreds of seminars and workshops on career and life plateauing, and I always ask people "What do you require from your work to feel satisfied?" People are encouraged to call out their responses, and time after time they tend to name the same things. No matter what type of organization or industry, whether I'm talking to managers or professionals or line workers, there's tremendous consistency in what people say. Three conditions are needed in order for employees to feel enriched:

Challenge: To risk and learn and fulfill their potential
Empowerment: To be autonomous so they can be creative, make decisions, and act
Significance: To do things that matter and create value

These are also the three ingredients of Earning. In companies where a psychology of Earning exists, people have what they need to do good work. Thus, the task of leaders and managers is to nurture and maintain those three ingredients. (Specific techniques are presented in Chapter 8; for now, I simply want to point out the link between job satisfaction and the psychology of Earning.)

Challenge

People describe what challenge means to them in these words:

"I want to keep on learning."
"I want to use my talents."
"I want different responsibilities."
"I want to feel like I'm fulfilling my potential."
"I want every day to be different."
"I want to master new things."
"I want to keep on growing."
"I want some risk."
"I want it to be fun!"

To get commitment and high performance, organizations must make sure employees have the chance to tackle challenging experiences in which they stretch, learn, risk—and succeed.

Empowerment

When people describe what empowerment means to them, they say:

"I want to make decisions."
"I need to be autonomous."
"I want to be able to act."
"I like to be on the leading edge."
"I need to be creative."
"I want to innovate."
"I need to lead."
"I want people to respect me."
"I want authority."
"I need flexibility."
"I don't want to have to ask permission."
"I don't want to have to go by the book."
"I want to be responsible."
"I want to be accountable."

When people are given opportunities to organize and make decisions appropriate to their knowledge and experience, they usually move up to the opportunity. They think of themselves, they sharpen their skills, they focus their efforts, and they display grit and self-control. Given the chance, freed from the restrictions of the hierarchy, sustained by the group, they move further into the psychology of Earning.

The payoff for organizations is tremendous. Jack Welch, the CEO of General Electric, says "If we let our people flourish and grow, if we use the best ideas they come up with, then we have the chance to win [in global competition]. The idea of liberation and empowerment for our work force is not enlightenment—it's a competitive necessity."

Significance

Most people want their work to be significant. They're asking that their work contribute to something they feel is important:

> "I want to do things that matter."
> "I want to feel I've achieved, I've accomplished, I've made a difference."
> "I want excellence."
> "I need to create value."
> "What I do is important work."
> "I don't just shuffle paper."
> "I'm in the mainstream."
> "I make an impact."
> "There's a purpose to what I do."
> "I'm contributing to something important."
> "My work makes me feel like I'm a good person."

In an interview in *Harvard Business Review,* Paul Cook, CEO of Raychem Corporation, was asked how he keeps his people motivated over the long haul:

> Most people, whether they're engineers, business managers, or machine operators, want to be creative.

They want to identify with the success of their profession and their organization. They want to contribute to giving society more comfort, better health, more excitement. And their greatest reward is receiving acknowledgment that they did contribute to making something meaningful happen. So the most important thing we do is build an organization—a culture, if you'll pardon the word—that encourages teamwork, that encourages fun and excitement, that encourages everyone to do things differently and better—and that acknowledges and rewards people who excel.

Creating an Organization of Winners

Psychological research tells us that motivation is highest when the probability of success is 50 percent: We don't get involved if the task is too easy or too hard. At its core, then, creating the conditions of Earning means moving people into a middle range of risk—increasing pressure if people are stuck in Entitlement, or decreasing pressure if they are paralyzed by Fear—while supporting their efforts.

Reaching that middle point may take a significant push. Since nothing is more confidence-building than facing risk directly and managing it, people who avoid risk have to be required to move into it. If organizations don't require the stretch, people can be cheated of the sense of accomplishment that comes from pushing beyond what's comfortable.

The goal is not to create Fear, which would be unproductive. Rather it is that medium level of risk that stimulates achievement. That's why clever organizations continuously increase the requirements of performance. If you set those goals within the reach of a stretch, the negative pressure has a positive outcome because the level of accomplishment becomes a triumph. IBM calls it "raising the bar" and the targets are set so that 90 percent of the people can attain them.

To illustrate the effective use of anxiety leading to success, my favorite example is the boot camp training of the Marine

Corps. (I'm not prescribing military service. I'm simply observing the Marine Corps' very successful use of manageable anxiety to achieve a goal.)

San Diego is home for one of the largest boot camps of the Corps. Whenever I fly home, there are always some Marine recruits on the plane. Adolescents, they come in many assorted and ill-fitted sizes: skinny and weak, fat and sloppy, pimply and awkward. I look at these kids and I think, "*You* are going to defend me?" Twelve weeks later they are not recognizable. They stand tall. They walk with controlled power. They project confidence. The change is awesome.

How do the Marines do it? The drill instructor (DI) pushes as hard as possible, using as much top-down power, as much authority, as possible. That amount of authority takes the recruits into very high levels of anxiety. In our model, they go into Fear. But the Marine Corps has also created the mechanism by which the Boots can earn their way out of anxiety.

The DI teaches the recruits not to fail the platoon. Under the conditions of Fear, the recruits are offered a hand: If they relate to each other, if they bond together, if each individual's loyalty is to the unit, then each individual has access to support from the whole group when needed.

The Marines use fear and competition to create high anxiety. They use high anxiety to create bonding. The bonding results both in peer support and peer pressure to perform. The combined peer support and pressure result in high performance. High performance creates the sense of being empowered, of being confident. Sustained empowerment and performance result in a psychology of Earning. What a training program!

5

Understanding How People Work—The Earning Curve

Everything discussed so far can be summarized in one simple drawing. If we make a graph with productivity on one plane and pressure (anxiety, risk, stress, fear—here they all mean the same) on the other, and draw in the familiar bell-shaped curve (see Fig. 5-1), we can see how productivity and anxiety relate:

Productivity is very low when the level of stress is either very low or very high.

The graph is what social scientists call a model—a way of displaying relationships in visual format. I developed the model from my observations about how people behave and also from two other sources.

The first is the Yerkes-Dodson law, sometimes cited as the only example of a really scientific psychological law, stating that "Anxiety improves performance until a certain optimum level of arousal has been reached. Beyond that point, performance deteriorates as higher levels of anxiety are attained."

The second source is the research done by David Mc-Clelland of Harvard University and John Atkinson of the University of Michigan. They found that motivation to achieve and level of effort keep rising until the expectancy of success (or the level of uncertainty) reaches 50 percent. Then, even though the expectancy continues to increase, motivation falls. When

Figure 5-1. Levels of productivity as a response to anxiety.

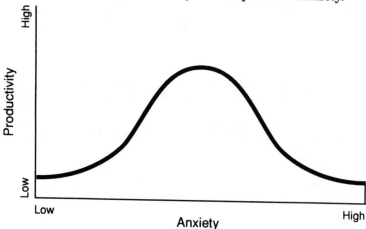

the goal is seen as too easy (too certain) or too difficult (too uncertain), there is no motivation or effort.

Though they're not discussing exactly the same variables, these two models converge: The relationships they're describing can be drawn as bell-shaped curves.

If we then superimpose the three psychological conditions on our basic bell curve graph, we get Figure 5-2. On the left

Figure 5-2. Entitlement, Earning, and Fear.

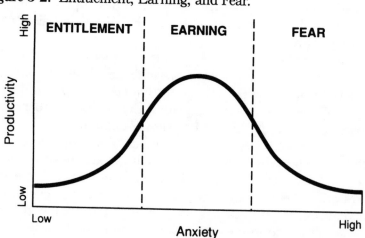

side of the curve, anxiety is very low and productivity is very low. This is the Entitlement section of the graph. In the center section, anxiety is moderate and productivity is highest. This section represents the psychology of Earning. On the right side of the graph, anxiety is very high and productivity is very low. This section describes the psychology of Fear.

We will come back to this three-segment curve and will add another layer of information, but first I want to present another way to understand the relationship between anxiety and productivity. In Figure 5-3, the behaviors that you might see under the three different conditions are presented as a kind of verbal profile.

Nine Points on the Earning Curve

Now we can take the model one step further and identify more closely where a person or an organization is on the spectrum. Using a curve makes us realize there are degrees of the psychological states. This is true whether we're talking about an individual in an organization or an organization as a whole. I have assigned numbers to areas along the curve (see Fig. 5-4). Throughout the rest of the book you'll find these numbers, for example:

> "I think I'm a 4."
> "That company is a 7."
> "My first supervisor was a 2."

The numbers are a relative measure of where an item is on the scale.

As complex as a model may appear, reality is always much more complicated because people or institutions are rarely pure examples of a single state. Instead, you'll usually find they have a strong central tendency that is akin to one place on our curve, and also other aspects of attitudes or behaviors that are closer to other places. Nonetheless, it is possible to generalize about each of the nine points and to describe what they are like.

The descriptions are divided into two general categories:

Figure 5-3. The Earning curve as a verbal profile.

WHAT ENTITLEMENT LOOKS LIKE

High Levels	*Low Levels*
Risk avoidance	Flexibility
Avoiding assessment	Accountability
Dependence, passivity	Morale and motivation
Apathy, complacency	Firing
Conformity, rule following	Innovation
Bureaucracy	Empowerment
High number of rules and procedures	Evaluation
High number of rule checkers	Confidence in subordinates

Bottom line: Avoiding risk and creating safety are institutionalized in rules and procedures. Appearance is more important than achievement.

WHAT EARNING LOOKS LIKE

Low Levels	*High Levels*
Self-protection	Trust
Apathy	Accountability
Dependence	Innovation
Following precedent	Leadership
Passivity	Risk taking
	Involvement
	Teamwork
	Decision making
	Motivation
	Excitement

Bottom line: The motive to achieve is high because achieving is possible and security depends on producing.

WHAT FEAR LOOKS LIKE

Low Levels	*High Levels*
Security	Anxiety, uncertainty
Control	Despair

(continued)

Figure 5-3. (*continued*).

Low Levels	*High Levels*
Morale	Stress
Teamwork	Self-protection
Trust	Dependence
Respect for leaders	Cynicism
Citizenship behavior	Turf protecting
	Denial
	Vulnerability

Bottom line: There is no sense of having any control. People panic and it's every person for himself.

---

what organizations are like at the nine points and what individuals are like at those same points. As you will see when we begin developing a strategy for change, it is important to be clear whether the problem involves an organization or a group of individuals.

What Organizations Are Like

Point 1. Very hard to fire people. Enforcing discipline takes lots of written justification. Promotion mostly based on seniority. Many hierarchical levels. A hierarchical culture in which formal status is extremely important. No risk taking. Many rules. More emphasis on process or procedure than outcome. Lots of paper. Lots of people checking on others. Many studies and pilot efforts. No new decisions. All the time in the world. No energy. Apathy. Precedent is holy. Respect really means Entitlement.

Point 2. Evaluations too positive. Excess graciousness. No disagreements or confrontations. Little distinction in pay between high and low performers. Looking busy is highly valued so there's lots of face time. Empowerment and risk taking are rare. Committees advise but don't decide. Decisions handed up. Emphasis on what people are owed rather than on what they owe. A culture of assumption and precedent. Do it "our way."

Figure 5-4. The Earning curve.

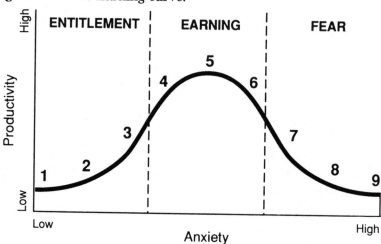

Point 3. Informal tenure for everyone. People compete for success but without obvious drive; style is important. Exchanges usually mannered and gracious. Some empowerment but with a leash. Status differences important though lots of work organized in small groups. Little risk-taking. Progress predictable and incremental. Breakthroughs rare so small innovations treated as big deals. Decisions require management sign-off. Criticism of the organization but not enough of a sense of imperative so that significant changes are made. Basically, it's comfortable.

Point 4. Innovators respected but formal position in the hierarchy remains important as a determinant of influence. Impersonal, creative confrontation or probing discussions. Much work organized in teams. Peer pressure important. Decisions typically made by consensus. Time given to analyze and plan. Change typically thoughtful, logical, and incremental. Mood calm but involved.

Point 5. Few levels of the hierarchy. Dynamics of most relationships like those of peers. Many autonomous teams. Few rules; considerable flexibility. Creativity rewarded. Evaluations cover the full range. Significant rewards and punishments according to performance. Organization is performance (or customer) driven. Outcome much more important than process but procedure has a place. A meritocracy; there are many kinds of power. There's trust. Channels of communication are open. Energy of forward momentum toward a successful future; a sense of excitement.

Point 6. There are two different ways organizations function at point 6. In one case, it is the result of uncertainty and risk: There's a lot of challenge in the environment so some elements of security can't be taken for granted, or there's enormous pressure from superiors and peers to perform. In this case, people are very visible in terms of performance and pressure to perform is unremitting. Errors are punished but not as much as not doing one's best. Work comes first. It's assumed to be the most important thing in everyone's life.

The second way is to be an organization that enjoys and prefers to be in a riskier or more entrepreneurial mode. The greatest prestige goes to innovators and creators. Knowledge is power and it's more important than formal status. Evaluations are tough and there are significant rewards and punishments. Decisions are made both by consensus and unilaterally. The pace of change is fast. With few rules, there's little regard for precedent. Deviance is applauded. It's a procedurally or structurally loose organization and it works. The mood is that of high excitement.

Point 7. Discomfort because no one knows the right way to do things. Decisions are pushed up. Efforts made to generate new, more appropriate rules or procedures. Discussion of the future and efforts to create the new vision. Doubt about the future, some skepticism that it can be made to work, some putting down of the leadership, but also some hope. Some of the better people may be leaving. The pendulum of values and goals moves in arcs that are too wide because the preference is for action and there's impatience when solutions are not achieved quickly. High energy level. Tendency to overreact and therefore act precipitously.

Point 8. No sense of security or predictability. Leaders are not leading. Rules and precedents from the past are rarely appropriate now, but there aren't any clear new ones. A lot of floundering. The result is attempts to grab new rules (or a vision or a culture) from somewhere rather than let them evolve. Discussion of future goals but the goals or vision are discounted. Poor morale. Communication is top-down. Decisions rarely made and less frequently implemented. Mood is cynical.

Point 9. Rules from the past in a present that is chaos. No rules that work. No vision, strategy, or leadership. As a result, there's clinging to precedent, old rules, and conforming in the bureaucracy. Decisions are made. No focus. There's either the high energy of panic or the flatness of fatalism. Terrible morale.

Figure 5-5 is an overview of the nine points on the curve as it applies to organizations.

In the same way that we characterized organizations, we can describe the nine facets of the curve as they might be reflected in an individual.

Figure 5-5. Summary of points on the Earning curve for organizations.

Point	Characteristic
1.	A PRECEDENT-DRIVEN BUREAUCRACY that has all the time in the world.
2.	A PSEUDOMERITOCRACY of inconsequential evaluations.
3.	A sense of COMFORT within GRACIOUS COMPETITION.
4.	Incremental progress through TEAMS and CONSENSUAL DECISION-MAKING.
5.	EXCELLENCE achieved through CONTINUOUS ADAPTATION to the REALITIES of OUTCOME.
6.	INNOVATION, CREATIVITY, and RISK TAKING get the highest marks.
7.	OVERREACTING, goals and values CHANGE in BIG ARCS.
8.	In crisis, LEADERS and the FUTURE are viewed CYNICALLY.
9.	WITHOUT GOALS or LEADERSHIP the present and future feel OUT OF CONTROL.

What Individuals Are Like

Point 1. *I have it coming because you owe me.* Panics with risk. Emotion high if there is the perception of any risk, including that of accountability. With risk, this person needs a life-saver. Tendency to deny the loss of entitlement or the requirement for performance. Follows and memorizes the rules. Avoids risk. Apathetic, passive, and dependent though that can be hard to discern under the overt "You owe me" attitude. Intervention is tricky because, with the perception of risk, this person is prone to go from 1 to 9.

Point 2. *I did the best I could so I don't understand why you're crabbing at me.* Resistant to increased risk or accountability. Projects causes from the self and rationalizes failure: "Circumstances were out of my control." May say "This is good enough." Blames others—managers or co-workers—for nonperformance. Very judgmental and frequently verbal. Presumptuous. Greedy. Avoids assessment. Tries to look good. Is prone to justify performance, saying "Look at the time and effort I put in!" Very difficult and time-consuming to deal with because the anxiety is high but so is the denial of any responsibility. Hard to budge from Entitlement.

Point 3. *I can see that things could be better, but you know, I'm really comfortable just the way they are.* Most of these people have had at least some success on the job. They'll accept what they perceive as a reasonable challenge, change, or incremental responsibility. It's not too hard to get their understanding. But, nonetheless, their strategy is to not make waves, keep things agreeable, placate the boss, and resist real change, including accountability. While they give lip service to the need for improvement, basically they're complacent. They'd like to keep things as they are.

Point 4. *Change is good, but haste gets you in trouble. Take the time to think things through.* These people work well, know they're competent, aren't afraid of change, but prefer to study the situation from many different angles before proceeding. Comfortable disagreeing with others in discussion, but prefer consensus rather than dictating to others. Prefer working with others and organize in teams.

Point 5. *I'm doing this as well as I can. There's only one standard of performance, and that's doing one's best. I can't help it—I'm naturally competitive. I go for excellence!* These people have attitudes, behaviors, and confidence that are optimal. As a result, they're flexible and adaptive. Aware of precedent but keep on learning. Disciplined in the pursuit of achievement. Responsible; autonomous and collaborative in turn, depending on circumstances. Initiating and decisive but trusting. Listen to others. Tell the truth. Optimistic, they're goal- and future-oriented.

Point 6. *I don't like doing things in dribs and drabs. When there's a need to do it, then do it! It's really fun to go out and hook horns with the big guys. If there's a chance, I'd rather go for the big one!* These people seek risk and may even create it. Dislike the assumption that following the rules is best. Comfortable deviating and my be creative. Often prefer to work alone, at least in analyzing or planning, and join with others only for implementation.

Point 7. *There's so much going on, there's so much coming down, you don't know what's going to happen. You can't let your guard down and you can never let up.* Too competitive, uneasy and stressed, this person isn't a good team player. Though too tense for optimal performance, not far from the success pattern. Need reassurance. In this case, the reassurance most needed is that they can meet challenge, they can succeed, and when they do, they'll regain a sense of having control over what's happening. Relatively easy to reassure.

Point 8. *Things are really scary out there. You can't trust anyone. What kind of lies am I being fed? You better be prepared. You better watch out!* This person grabs territory (i.e., budget and head count) and gets political (i.e., seeks power and supporters). Judgmental and emotional; blames the leadership (or parents). "Everything was better before." Narcissistic, cynical, and mistrustful. Hard to deal with. Time-consuming. Underlying his or her fears, there's often rage.

Point 9. *It's so awful that I can't think about this. It's so terrible, there's no way out. There's nothing I can do. Help me, help me! Make me safe.* There's so much fear that it's become a generalized anxiety; a pervasive sense of doom. People are often paralyzed, incapable of doing anything purposeful. Cling to what they've already mastered; survive by scooting along the top of reality, never looking at it, never dealing with it. Self-preoccupied, there's a constant search for support and reassurance. Whatever the overt behavior, there's panic. Intervention is crucial. Offered a hand, they may cling like a limpet.

Figure 5-6 summarizes these levels.

Try your hand at the model; it's fun, and it will help solidify the concept. For example, where would you put:

> United States? (in my workshops, usually 2 or 3)
> Japan? (usually 4 or 5)
> Your company?
> Your part of the business?
> Your boss?
> Your direct reports?
> The person at the next desk?
> Yourself?

Mismatch Between Individuals and Companies

We have to distinguish between where an organization might be on the Earning curve and where individuals are. The level of

Figure 5-6. Attitudes on the Earning curve.

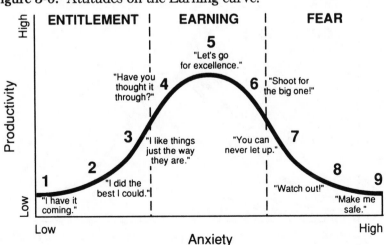

anxiety present in the culture of any organization will affect the uncertainty of the individuals within it, but not all individuals will have the same level of anxiety. While there may be conditions that create an overall psychology of Entitlement, individuals within those circumstances may have a psychology of Earning or even of Fear.

There are large differences in how people experience risk. Some people find small amounts of risk very scary, very threatening to their sense of well-being. It would not take much change for them to go from Entitlement to Fear. Other people are much more comfortable with some levels of uncertainty or risk. People who put challenge high on their list of requirements for personal satisfaction are less likely to be panicked when there's a moderate increase in uncertainty. And finally, there are a small number of people who enjoy risk and who create it when their lives become too predictable.

If we were to graph the experiences of individuals within an organization, particularly an organization in significant transition, we would have separate and disjointed waves; see Figure 5-7.

Paradoxically, many organizations that are deepest into Entitlement will attract individuals who are most interested in Earning. Entitled organizations include many of our most fa-

Figure 5-7. Anxiety amounts experienced by individuals.

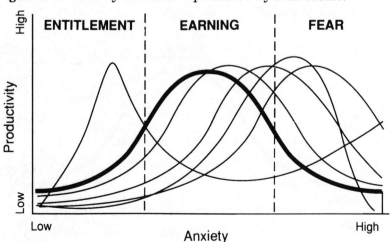

mous companies that have enormous resources and typically pay exceedingly well. They have always attracted very bright people, many of whom are highly motivated to achieve and compete. I've had these employees say to me "I'm a 5. I always look for a manager who's a 6, so I'll always have to stretch. What really worries me, and I don't think I could handle it, is if I had to work for a 2."

Those inner-directed, results-oriented people do not fit into that organization's culture of Entitlement. Usually, one of three things happens: (1) They become terribly frustrated and leave. (2) If they stay, they will plateau early because they don't fit in. (3) They may adopt to the institution's culture, retaining their ambition but losing their capacity to initiate and take risks.

Once in a while we see individuals who can retain an Earning mind-set within conditions of Entitlement, but that's not very likely if they remain within those conditions for long. If they do manage to keep their Earning psychology, it's probably because they have had at least some occasional real challenges and demands for high performance within the organization, or they are having those experiences somewhere else in their life.

When there is a large gap between the institutional and the individual comfort level with risk (see Fig. 5-8), the best choice is usually for the individual to leave. It's very difficult to move

Figure 5-8. Misfit between the individual and the organization.

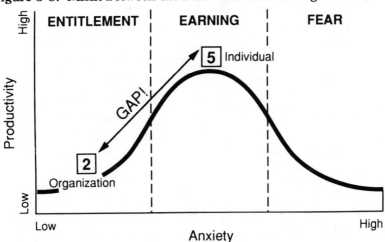

an organization by yourself; it's tragic to give up an esteemed part of yourself.

Making Changes

Let's assume that we now understand the three psychological states and their consequences in human behaviors. With the model, we have a tool for measuring the three conditions. Now, how do we make use of this understanding to improve our organizations? How will we get to a psychology of Earning if we are not there already? In a deliberate and constructive way, we have to use risk. Looking at your organization, consider these questions:

- Why should we change? What is there in the environment that creates the urgency?
- What core changes are needed? What are the biggest issues?
- Where should we start? What do we focus on? The organization? A division? An individual?
- Where are we on the curve? Which direction do we need to go in?
- What's our basic strategy for moving from one state to another? Do we know enough about the possible techniques?
- Who is in charge of the change? We'll need to identify individuals or a team with clear responsibilities.
- How will we protect the innovators of change? Do we need mechanisms for group evaluations and decisions?
- What's in it for the individual who changes?
- What happens to individuals who don't change?
- What will we tell everyone?

Assuming change is needed (the first two items), what's the process of bringing it about?

What Kind of Problem?

The first step is to be clear about what you are dealing with. Is the problem an organizational one or does it involve one or more individuals? That will tell you whether you need an organizational policy or an individual intervention.

Executives and top-level managers will probably be concerned with the entire organization as one entity. They should watch for variations within that one entity. Some people within the organization, as individuals, will fall at different points from where the organization as a whole falls. If the environment involves a merger or acquisition of organizations with different cultures, there can be differences on a very large scale.

Mid-level managers, shop supervisors, managers of work units or teams, and anyone else who is responsible for the performance of more than a few people will also probably start with a focus on the organization, although the organization in question will be much smaller (perhaps a department or work group) and individual differences may assume greater importance.

Those concerned with the performance and work attitudes of one or a few people will look toward the descriptions for individuals. Here is also where you will focus if you are wise enough to see the need for change in yourself and are brave enough to tackle it.

Which Direction?

Next to be considered is "Where are we (if this is an organizational problem) on the Earning curve?" Or, if you're focused at the individual level, "Where is this person on the curve?" Remember that your goal is to be at the midpoint, where the best work gets done. To move to that point, you may have to increase pressure or decrease it. Once you know where the organization or the individual is on the curve, you know in which direction you have to move.

As best you can, assess the current conditions using the descriptions of the nine phases. This assessment involves two

tasks. You have to monitor behavior and, since the critical variable is an emotion, you must also trust how it feels. On either
the organizational or the individual level, observe what people
do and monitor how these actions *feel*. Be as exact as possible,
which is seldom easy. For one thing, as we mentioned earlier,
people and companies rarely fit neatly into just one category.

- If you see lots of long hours but nothing much is
achieved, if there's lots of bureaucratic caution, and if people
never challenge each other, chances are good that the emotional climate is flat and apathetic. Then you're in Entitlement.
(*Caution:* Where Entitlement is extreme, so is denial. In that
case, outside observers are probably necessary both to assess the
core state and to strategize for change.)

- If no work is getting done because people are paralyzed
by panic or preoccupied with protecting their own turf; if you
sense a climate of depression, cynicism, and mistrust; and if
people seem narcissistic and grasping, chances are you're in
Fear.

- If work is being produced and people are optimistic,
gutsy, energetic, involved, excited, and oriented to the future,
you're in Earning.

What Strategy?

Once you know in which direction to move, you can begin
to plan your strategy for orchestrating change. In general
terms, the overall approaches for each condition are:

- If your assessment shows that the mood is primarily one
of Entitlement, some level of tension must be constructed.
That's done by creating significant positive or negative outcomes as a result of performance. For example, "If we don't hit
our targets, no one gets a bonus."

- If you determine that the mood is overly anxious, then
you must take steps to reduce anxiety. Be straight about what
is happening and what people can expect; don't leave any room

for rumors. Emphasize successes and historic stability. Strive for calm.

• If you have a condition of Earning, your goal is to maintain and nurture it, with perhaps a little fine-tuning to make it even better. Your biggest danger is that you'll increase or decrease the risk level when it's not needed and take people into a less optimal part of the curve.

What Next?

In all cases, the generalized states have to be converted to specific problems or issues that lend themselves to being managed. For example, the core issues in Entitlement are often things like a weighty bureaucracy with too many rules, a culture that resists innovation, or a lack of confidence in subordinates. Those are awfully big institutional issues. More progress is likely if they can be transformed into smaller and specific tasks such as "Let's cut out levels of management, go through the manuals and cut out rules, and be sure everyone knows they can't send decisions up."

The next three chapters consider that specifics of change. For both individuals and organizations, strategies for each of the nine points on the curve are described and many specific techniques are presented. If you are in Entitlement, turn to Chapter 6. If you are in Fear, turn to Chapter 7. If you are in Earning, turn to Chapter 8.

Whenever the goal is to change the organization, it's necessary that the reasons for change be articulated very clearly. Because understanding always facilitates change, executives and managers need to tell people what they're trying to accomplish and why.

Organizational change from one set of values to another can easily take from three to five years. But taking no action will jeopardize the very survival of your organization.

6

Moving Away From Entitlement—Increase Pressure

The only way to energize lethargic organizations and people is to push them into the psychology of Earning. It usually takes some shaking up—perhaps even a crisis. But after years of avoiding risk, people find any risk frightening. It is important to remember that when there is a lot of Entitlement, any movement toward Earning, even if it is small, feels like Fear at first. That's why we say that any movement out of deep Entitlement toward Earning always means moving first into Fear. And that's precisely why it's so hard.

Naturally, people resist leaving the comfort of Entitlement. When they're pushed out of it, they will try to return. Even managers have a tendency to return to the bureaucratic security of Entitlement as soon as the latest crisis is past. This rebound effect is inevitable; people always tend to slide backward. That's why continued pressure is needed to make the changes stick.

Senior managers will need great courage and toughness. It takes courage to sustain the pressure long enough so people truly realize Entitlement is over. The period of change will inevitably be a time of low morale: Expect lots of complaining, delaying, and resisting (see Fig. 6-1, which displays the full process). Drastic measures may be called for. A new vision will not take people into Earning; more than a carrot, you will need a stick.

Figure 6-1. Using stress to create excitement.

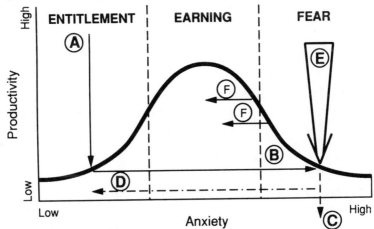

(A) Performance is required.
(B) From Entitlement to Fear.
(C) Morale plunges.
(D) Efforts are made to return to Entitlement.
(E) Despite lowered morale, requirements for performance are sustained.
(F) Only in this way do people and organizations learn that the only way to reduce anxiety is to earn your way out.

Only pressure takes people and organizations out of Entitlement. But pressure is only half the prescription; the other half is support. Apply pressure while applying support. Pressure takes the form of required achievement; support takes the form of information, counseling, and tools.

You must be careful not to exert so much pressure that people go to the extreme right of the curve, into panic. The longer people and organizations remain in the high-anxiety sector, the more fearful they will become. Then you have the opposite problem: Rather than being complacent, people are too paralyzed to work.

Three Overall Approaches

In this chapter we examine ways to counteract the conditions of Entitlement. We use two phases. First, as a kind of overview, we revisit the first three points of the Earning curve, the Entitlement section:

Point 1:	Confront with support.
Point 2:	Confront.
Point 3:	Challenge.

These strategies take slightly different forms, depending on whether the affected group is an entire organization or one or more individuals.

When it is the entire organization that needs changing, the driving force must be the top leaders. They must be prepared to maintain pressure, encourage attempts, tolerate mistakes, and reward achievements. More specifically, there are three overall strategies for organizational change, one for each of the three Entitlement points on the curve. They are summarized in the sidebar.

Entitled Organizations: What Executives Should Do

Point 1. *Confront with support.* The focus is on increasing accountability. The message to be communicated throughout the organization is "We waste too much time and energy on things that aren't important. We have to get things in focus. If we don't get more stuff out, and faster, we're in big trouble. Let's figure out what really counts."

Point 2. *Confront.* The focus is on evaluation. The message from the top should be: "Our evaluations are too high. Everyone gets graded 'outstanding,' but we have people who don't pull their weight and we have others who do the work of three. From now on everyone's going to be ranked. There's going to be no more hiding."

Point 3. *Challenge.* The organization's focus should be on *pushing power down.* The message to be communicated is

"Things are too comfortable around here. From now on we expect everyone to have an opinion and we're going to ask for it. We expect everyone to defend their point of view. We want to hear a lot more from the people who actually do the work. Managers and supervisors, you are to talk less, listen more, and require participation."

If the focus of attention is a smaller unit—even one person—the overall techniques are the same, but they show themselves in slightly different ways. For managers working with individuals, it is often a question of how best to motivate (see the sidebar).

Entitled Individuals: What Managers Should Do

Point 1. *Confront with support.* Be very clear about requiring performance and be specific. Provide a time when the job is to be completed and keep it short—no more than a week. Verbalize your availability for help. Say something like "This is exactly what I want you to do. You have two days to do it. Remember, if you have any trouble with this, I want you to come to me and I'll help. I'm here if you need me."

Point 2. *Confront.* Increase the conditionality of receiving rewards. Provide short to medium time parameters. "This is your assignment. I want it ready for my review by noon on Friday. That's four days from now. I expect to see a significant improvement in accuracy over your last two assignments. If I don't get it, you're not earning your salary."

Point 3. *Challenge.* Motivate this person by communicating an attitude of "You're capable of doing significantly better work. I'm confident you can do it. I expect much more from you." Sustain pressure. Use constructive competition. Being a member of the team has to be earned.

Using Pressure to Increase Productivity: Seven Strategies

Here are seven specific techniques for deliberately increasing the anxiety level. Although all could be used at any level in the Entitlement portion of the curve, they are particularly appropriate to one particular level, noted in the number in parentheses:

1. Increase accountability through evaluation (level 1).
2. Require ongoing risk-taking (level 1).
3. Increase visibility and peer pressure; flatten the hierarchy (level 2).
4. Increase conditionality and reward differentially (level 2).
5. Visibly fire for nonperformance (level 2).
6. Create competition (level 3).
7. Assure a meritocracy (level 3).

Remember that real situations are usually complicated, because pure types are rare. In addition, as we create change, we cannot know absolutely what the outcome will be. We can strategize and plan changes, but in reality the change that occurs may be only an approximation of our plan. Trying, fixing, and adapting are always necessary.

Many of these techniques are interconnected: Organizations may be structured in such a way that these various techniques occur in a natural flow from one to the next. That is, when you increase peer pressure, you are at the same time creating the conditions of meritocracy. When you push power down by flattening a hierarchy, you automatically increase accountability. And when you formulate a reward system that is linked to that accountability, you have increased conditionality ("You don't get the reward unless you do what we hold you accountable for") and you are also rewarding differentially (strong producers get more than weak producers.)

Whirlpool shows how strategies can be linked. CEO David Whitman says "We have a new organizational structure and have pushed accountability into that structure much more. We put in place a bonus plan which allows better monitoring of performance and provides greater incentives."

Increase Accountability Through Evaluations

People need to be held accountable for doing real work and that work must be evaluated. The accountability must be in terms of the core, or most important parts, of a person's responsibilities. That is, identify what is real work and decide how to evaluate it. Then reinforce those evaluations by tying compensation to performance. Performance must be sharply differentiated from the amount of time people work. People need to be continually asked "What value do you add?"

What Is Real Work?

The organization needs an objective and systematic review of jobs, analyzing the value of assignments and differentiating between core and peripheral tasks. This process requires that managers be clear about what really needs to be accomplished. Take the time to think through what the essential business of the company is and therefore what constitutes real work or significant added value.

Periodically all units should initiate a major review, seeking to answer: What business are we really in? What work is really important? What work (and employees) are redundant or superfluous? How excellent are we? Are we preparing for the future? Insist that all workers be directly involved in the analysis; for example, ask them: "If you had 20 percent less (or more) time, how would you change your job? If you could, how would you redesign your job?"

The purpose of this review is to determine what people (or the unit) should focus on and be held most accountable for. We have to discriminate between putting in time and achieving something significant. Being busy is not the same as being productive. Creating mountains of elegant paper is not the same as adding value. Measure people's performance—what they actually contribute. This measurement will require clear, attainable, and worthwhile goals.

In 1990, Oryx, a Texas oil and gas producer, saved $70 million by getting rid of procedures, reviews, reports, and approvals that had little to do with discovering oil, which is the company's *real* work. Three years earlier, after dropping 1,500 positions, Oryx found its costs were still too high. A consulting firm surveyed the remaining employees and discovered they were concentrating mostly on meeting budget targets, not on locating oil.

Oryx set up teams of employees from all departments to identify unnecessary work. Following the teams' recommendations, the company discontinued 25 percent of all internal reports, decided that four signatures on requests for capital expenditures were enough (not twenty), and found ways to produce the annual budget in six weeks instead of seven months. Over the next two years, Oryx cut another 1,500 jobs, mostly middle managers whose work had largely been eliminated. Now the company is replacing its oil reserves twice as fast at half the cost.

As the Oryx experience demonstrates, the tough examination of job content is especially important when some downsizing has occurred. Many companies have cut so they have a leaner structure, but after they downsized, they didn't reduce the work load. You have to constantly look at people's work and ask "Is this necessary? Is it important to the mission? To the customer?" You have to prioritize. You probably need to relearn that great word, "No." Cut paper work; don't document things to death. Eliminate work that doesn't really contribute and get people to do the critical tasks. Work should emphasize what must be done, not what would be nice to have.

Addressing the process by which work gets done, as well as identifying what actually constitutes *work,* has become extremely important, because downsizing by itself may leave layers of management in place so that decision-making remains slow and coordination between functions remains problematic. Efforts to achieve significantly higher levels of efficiency and productivity include total quality management, reengineering, business-process redesign, and creating a horizontal organization. The trend is toward flatter organizations in which work is increasingly structured around a few core processes rather than departments or functions. Successful change efforts begin by identifying the outcomes that are critical and then eliminating everything that's done that doesn't really contribute toward reaching the desired objectives.

Changes of this magnitude are difficult to achieve. Therefore, start evaluating the content of jobs in parts of the organization where discontent is high and satisfaction is low. People there may already be motivated to get things improved.

Evaluating Real Performance

There are several ways to make it easier to evaluate others and then communicate the evaluation. One is to use teams of evaluators. Individuals may feel uncomfortable judging others, but the pooled evaluation of several judges can be communicated with more confidence and greater impersonality than the estimate of one person. In this instance, procedures can be of great help. In many institutions, individual evaluations are the simultaneous responsibility of several people.

The organization should gather evaluations about people's performance from a range of superiors, peers, and subordinates regularly (e.g., every four to six months). Sometimes these evaluations are anonymous; this decision is up to company policy.

Since evaluations are usually skewed too positively, people who communicate evaluations need support in order to become more honest about negative input. That support can be created by having evaluation data from a range of other people, or having evaluations be the result of a consensus from a number of judges. That is, evaluation boards can be created and summary evaluations can be communicated by someone other than an individual's own manager.

Also, the evaluation procedure can be more comfortable for the evaluator if very detailed judgments are not required. When the range of ability is so narrow that people are very similar to each other, use only a few categories of performance.

Pushing fine distinctions when people have comparable abilities is difficult for the evaluators and demoralizing for the workers.

Many tasks are not easily quantified. In those cases, consider evaluation procedures that involve using several experts to evaluate the work performance. Together, they present their opinions to the person's manager. This group approach means that those making the assessment are also being judged, and therefore people in this situation tend to be careful and thoughtful in their evaluations.

Institute evaluation by peers and subordinates as well as by superiors. It's harder to impress a group of people than one person. Impressing a group tends to require performance; flattery won't help much. Also, the judgments of a group are harder to dismiss than the idiosyncrasies of an individual. Customer evaluations can be an additional source of pressure for accountability and an additional kind of information for determining compensation.

Reinforcing Real Performance Through Rewards

Accountability and the reward system must be intertwined. People need to have some of their rewards at risk in the sense that the reward can be gained only when they meet the specific and most important goals they are accountable for achieving. (The idea of differentiating rewards according to performance is discussed later in this chapter as a strategy in the section "Reward Differentially, Increase Conditionally.") Work will be organized in small groups in order to increase peer pressure (see strategy discussed in the section, "Increase Visibility and Peer Pressure"), but the largest percentage of the evaluation should be based on the group's performance (65 percent); the individual's performance should be a smaller portion (35 percent).

It is likely that pressure will have to be built into the evaluation system. Pressure has to bear on poor performers, so that if they remain poor performers, it will be uncomfortable for them and hard for them to stay in the company. Poor performers rarely improve, especially once they've developed an attitude of Entitlement, unless there are real consequences to performing or not.

The organization might start by using forced ranking with clearly different rewards for those at different percentiles. If that isn't enough pressure, if the organization is deep into Entitlement, clear and negative outcomes are required. For example, the bottom 5 percent could be put on probation; the bottom 6 to 15 percent would get neither a merit nor a cost of living salary increase. A forced distribution could be created in which only 5 percent can be exceptional, 25 percent are outstanding, 40 percent are average, 25 percent meet requirements, and 5 percent must be graded as unsatisfactory.

Require Ongoing Risk Taking

Since Entitlement is the result of too little risk, organizations should require that people experience challenge on an ongoing basis, even without a job change. People are not allowed to become or remain narrow experts nor are they permitted to become complacent, because new assignments require learning and risk taking.

Create opportunities for work challenge. Create an organizational policy of releasing people for new assignments. Stimulate more rotation assignments between line and staff. Unless the circumstances of the work, or the content of the responsibilities, or the interactions within the assignment are changing, no one should be allowed to continue doing the same work for more than three years because the most complex job is mastered within that time. An appropriate target is that every year, about 25 percent of people's assignments should be new to them.

At Toronto Dominion Bank, top management has decreed that the "new" bank will be a place where people will not be punished for taking risks. "What you should do," they are saying, "is actively look around this organization for opportunities to take on bigger responsibilities to make your job more exciting. Innovate. Do it!"

Policies should operate from the premise that people want the chance to meet challenge, master new skills, work through risks, innovate, make a difference, and lead. These policies have to become a working assumption, with the result that people take change for granted and view those who resist job change as deficient.

The definition of success will have to include the idea of earning different and sometimes more difficult assignments, with increasing levels of autonomy and decision-making responsibilities. Management should assume people can be largely responsible for themselves, can analyze and make decisions, and can initiate.

Increase Visibility and Peer Pressure

The key is to make people visible and you do that by flattening the hierarchy. People hide in the bureaucracy by handing decisions up, by creating committees. With a leaner and flatter structure, everyone is more visible. There aren't layers within which to hide.

Whenever possible, work should be assigned to small groups of people of similar status. The performance of the entire group will be evaluated, not the individual; this will increase the power of peer pressure to perform. It will also increase the bonding within the group, thus providing emotional support.

Though a flatter organization would appear to have fewer bosses and therefore less pressure to perform, people can be held responsible more easily when there's less of a hierarchy because it's harder to pass things on. In a flat organization, especially if the unit is a demarcated team with responsibility to produce, there'll be a lot of peer pressure on every individual to contribute, perform, and produce. It's much easier to hide from one boss than it is to be invisible to eight peers.

Peer pressure may be vastly more effective than any other kind. Peers can exert the pressure of accountability at the same time they support individuals.

Although performance is measured, for most people it's not necessary in terms of motivating them to perform. People feel responsible for achieving whatever their responsibilities are, partly because they know they'll be held accountable, but largely because they're in a milieu where people are unwilling to waste their time shuffling paper and evading responsibilities. People are willing to work very hard; they are not willing to have others around who don't.

While management monitors and evaluates performance, most of the work is handed off to reasonably autonomous teams composed of people of similar rank. Visibility and accountability are easier to achieve when units are made small. Organize so as to increase functional collaboration and mutual responsibility while keeping operating units small enough that players and their performance are visible to others. Nissan, for example, boasts of having the best attendance record in the United States, and that's without time clocks. It helps that Nissan's people are organized into teams of about twenty, so absentees are swiftly noticed. It further helps that Japanese plants are organized without relief workers. When someone's not present, the rest of the team members are supposed to pick up the slack.

Effective teams require input about decisions from everyone. Many groups are cross-functional or cross-skill teams, composed of people with a range of experiences and assumptions. For example, a new product design team could include people from engineering, manufacturing, sales, market research, and package design. In team meetings, all members simultaneously suggest issues from their own points of view. Their goal is to anticipate from the very beginning issues that could be important. This is in strong contrast to the traditional way of doing things, where engineering would design a product that manufacturing would then build with different specifications, and sales would be stuck trying to market a product that was different from what customers had been promised.

When the Honda Accord was being developed, the project manager held early brainstorming sessions with about a hundred people from many parts of the organization. Then, in line with Honda's tradition, these people developed two competing concepts of what the car might be like.

One important aspect of good teams is that they tend to foster innovative thinking. While all team members are expected to work cooperatively, it is also presumed that they will defend their divergent perspectives. I call it creative confrontation. It requires that people feel comfortable in disagreeing and that disagreement is not hostile. The objective is to develop superior solutions, which is most easily done in teams or task forces of peers who are cooperatively engaged and responsible.

Reward Differentially, Increase Conditionally

In most of our organizations, traditionally every job was classified and assigned a pay value. Despite the elaborate evaluation systems, there was little real variability in pay as a reflection of job performance. In these traditional systems, people get raises more or less automatically, either across the board (everyone gets a 6 percent increase every year) or when they move into a certain level of seniority (this is especially predominant in entitled organizations).

The situation is changing; people are beginning to be paid for contribution, not status. People come to realize that they can directly influence their rewards by how much they contribute. Those who make a greater contribution earn more and seniority has nothing to do with it.

People need to feel that they have an impact on what happens to them. That's why increasing numbers of companies are giving employees full financial information and saying "If we are profitable, you get a bonus." Rewards are possible, but there are conditions to be met.

The president of a general contracting firm opened the books to her seventy-two employees. Then she said "There will be no more raises. The only way people will be able to increase their money is by earning a bonus. Bonuses will depend on whether we're profitable." In addition to increased productivity, there was a marked decrease in costs. Before, no one had given any thought to calling long-distance during peak hours. Over time, the group became its own cost-cutting overseer.

Incentive Pay Plans

Incentive pay is critical. Without incentives for productivity, performance tends to slacken. Very simply, some amount of pay must be at risk when people are too comfortable.

When Warren Buffett, chairman of Berkshire Hathaway, acted as the interim chairman of Salomon Brothers he discovered to his dismay that 106 people who worked in the securities unit had each earned at least one million dollars in 1990, even though the division's results were below average that year. In response, Buffett wrote in a quarterly report that "Employees producing mediocre returns for owners should expect their pay to reflect this shortfall." All the managing directors used to be paid equally but now the top performers are paid up to twice as much as lesser performers.

Of course, there are many kinds of rewards, not all of them financial. Being a member of the winning team or being publicly recognized are extremely important rewards, but money is the most obvious. People may have difficulty in perceiving the reward value of varying opportunities to lead or make decisions, but they instantly perceive the difference between $5 and $500. Thus, some amount of money should be at risk.

Driven by increased competition and the need to improve performance, more and more organizations are increasing the variable component of pay. About 75 percent of American employers now have at least one kind of incentive pay plan and the great majority were installed after the 1981–82 recession when the permanent need to cut costs and increase productivity became clear.

Professor Ed Lawler of the University of Southern California is an expert on compensation. He recently said that "creative compensation plans generate some positive results in any era. Overall the results have been positive. Skill-based pay increases the cost per labor hour, but it has retention, quality, and loyalty benefits. Variable compensation plans—because they make payroll costs variable with company performance—show productivity effects."

The plans are not just for middle managers. At Borden, for example, some 28,000 workers at 180 different plants in 1990 had the chance to win bonuses ranging from $250 to $800 each, depending on how well their individual plants met various attendance, safety, quality, production, and financial goals.

Organizations like Allied-Signal are very aware that if they remove the security of people's pay they must give people the opportunity to earn more money. Their local labor leader, Ann Watkins of the UAW, said that "Management asked us to be more productive, and we wanted to know what was in it for us." On the one hand, Allied-Signal reduced the traditional annual raise from 3 percent to 2 at its spark-plug plant in Fostoria, Ohio. On the other hand, employees stood to gain as much as 6 percent if they met productivity improvement targets.

Even if the plant misses its productivity goals, the floor of the 2 percent raise is never in jeopardy. If productivity improves by 6 percent, people have earned a 3 percent increase. If productivity rises by 9 percent, the reward is a 6 percent raise. Formulas like this are increasing in popularity.

Some of the plans affect more than bonuses: Some portion of the base salary is also at risk. At Saturn, GM's new subsidiary, salaries are 80 percent of normal union scale; the rest is earned if workers reach productivity targets. If they do better than the targets, they earn more than 100 percent of their salary.

Monsanto has twenty-one different incentive plans, and thirteen of them link scheduled raises to performance. If they meet established goals, workers get the raise that is scheduled; if they exceed their goals, they get extra cash. "We used to focus on pay to attract, retain, and motivate," says Barry Bingham, Monsanto's corporate compensation director. "Now, we're using pay as a tool to drive results."

Planning Your Strategy

▪ *Involve employees in designing the program.* There is good evidence that the new pay systems do raise productivity. The effect may be greater when the organization has a significant amount of employee participation in decision making and employees have more responsibility and autonomy.

Greater involvement on the part of employees is almost certain to engender greater acceptance of the system. If the criteria of performance are obviously appropriate, and those making the evaluations are obviously credentialed, those who are judged as underproductive are likely to accept the evaluation. Equally important, employees are usually very angry when the reward system doesn't reflect differences in performance.

High performers are bitter about the lack of demonstrated appreciation for them and the fact that they're carrying underproductive people.

Organizations have to be careful to link the largest sector of the pay at risk with outcomes in which people are involved, responsible, and control. For example, a team bonus should be based on what the team achieved and not on the profitability of the entire organization.

■ *Include the entire organization, top to bottom.* Nonmanagement employees are not the only ones who have to have rewards at risk. Management at all levels must be part of the system too. Incentive pay is based on the notion that everyone's in the same boat. When anxiety and mistrust are high, it does not help that incentive pay is at risk in the ranks but the pay of CEOs bears little or no relation to company performance. The lack of a relationship is especially demoralizing when business is declining. When executives are exempt from the accountability that is imposed on everyone else, mistrust and bitterness are increased exponentially.

■ *Be prepared for initial resistance.* Where the system fostered Entitlement, any introduction of money at risk will be reacted to very negatively at first. A few years ago one of the regional Bell companies introduced a system of risk and bonuses. It set salaries at the seventy-fifth percentile of what the market was paying. Then management said "80 percent of your salary is a given; the other 20 percent is at risk. You may make more than the 20 percent if you are very productive and if we are profitable." Even though in the two years the system had operated people made more than the 20 percent in bonuses, they grumbled. And that was good: Management had to get their attention; it needed to communicate that the days of Entitlement were gone.

■ *Include punishment as well as reward.* Everyone has to know that failure to achieve has consequences. There has to be a real response to performance. In addition to the possibility of gaining rewards, there also has to be the possibility of some kind of punishment. Punishment may involve not getting bonuses or raises. It may be nonfinancial such as not being selected to participate in a leadership course. Whenever rewards are available, not getting can have more impact than getting. The range of punishment should also include something stronger such as being demoted or fired (see the strategy discussed in the next section, "Fire for Nonperformance").

■ *Assess your situation.* The need for differential rewards is clear, but there is a special case where rewards should not be differential: Whenever performance of individuals is roughly equal, imposing differentials is demotivating. In teams of highly skilled professionals selected for certain technical expertise, for instance, we would expect them all to be at approximately the same level of excellence. Surprisingly, however, using differentials is a fairly common practice in companies that use teams of highly selected professionals, because it is assumed that without that pressure, there will be little motivation to perform. Since professionals are usually highly motivated to begin with, this is really the imposition of demotivating punishment.

Fire for Nonperformance

Where Entitlement has a long history, people resist increases in pressure by denying that anything has changed. In the face of risk, they will hang on to Entitlement with the fiercest of embraces. It's necessary to get their attention, possibly by firing employees who don't perform.

I am not suggesting that firing be used arbitrarily. Those who are separated must clearly be underachieving and must have had an opportunity to increase their performance as a result of evaluation, guidance, and appropriate support. Then, if performance does not improve adequately, people should be fired.

In organizations of historic Entitlement, it will be a significant change in practice if not in policy. Those organizations usually have procedures by which people can be involuntarily separated from employment, but the procedures take endless time and endless paper.

The strategy here is to make it known throughout the organization that firing is indeed an option. Don't continue old euphemisms such as "decided to leave for personal reasons." Go public with the truth. Out of respect, don't use names, but include in periodic status reports a statement such as "Seven people left for regular retirement, twenty-three took early retirement, four left to other organizations, and six people were fired for inadequate performance."

Create Competition

The strategy here is to make competition continuous and important. People need to measure how they're doing all the time. It's especially useful to have an outside competitor, a villain to wage war against. If no outside villain is available, people may have to compete against their previous levels of performance, as their goals are raised; or the competition can be against other individuals, teams, units, or institutions.

Create a race against your competitive adversaries and keep score. Square D, which manufactures electrical equipment, put up a scoreboard on the outside wall of its headquarters building. Every day the board displays quarterly financial data: profit per employee, sales per employee, and return on equity for Square D compared to its main competitors—Emerson Electric, General Electric, and Westinghouse.

Personalizing an adversary can be energizing—the relationship between Coke and Pepsi springs to mind. As long as people are in the competition, it should be exciting and exhilarating. When employees are fighting against a common enemy, strong bonding occurs. Later, they will recall the years when they were competing for survival as the time when they had the most fun.

Keep raising your goals. As soon as you're near reaching the old goals, create big, new ones. Set performance targets that are stretch goals, but that 90 percent of the people will make. Then, the competition to reach the new goals is initially an enforced pressure for higher performance. As the goals are reached, the success is a positive experience.

Competition can be used to jar people out of Entitlement, especially when it's tied to differential rewards. We do not want to create a situation where a few people win and everyone else loses. The end point of the competition has to be a psychology of Earning and a sense of winning.

Create a Meritocracy

In a meritocracy, people at different levels of status, with different skills, styles, and backgrounds, can all earn the right to participate, influence, decide, lead, and succeed. All workers, at whatever hierarchical level, have an opportunity to demonstrate what they can do. Skill counts; status does not.

In a meritocracy, market forces prevail, in the sense that there is a continuous internal competition for increasing amounts of different kinds of power; one's hierarchical position is no protection from others' abilities and skills.

The idea is to create a culture in which subordinates expect to earn increasing decision-making power or autonomy and managers expect to delegate. This involves upward pressure from subordinates who presume their right to earn autonomy. The organizational caste system has to open to become a family of people who earned their entrance or their belonging.

The goal is the development of many leaders with a range of styles. Challenge by developing an organizational culture that makes it clear that "What's my job?" is the wrong question. People are continuously asked to instead answer "What's my function? What is the purpose of what I am doing? With that in mind, is there a better approach?"

Meritocracies enable the kind of creative confrontation we talked about earlier in this chapter. Searching, questioning, dissent, even conflict are givens. The confrontation may be heated, but it is not personal: There is too much respect for other people's abilities. Management must elicit opinions and then allow the differences to illuminate or lead to understanding. Executives and managers need to be trained to both collaborate and creatively confront employees in impersonal discussions so they model the behavior the organization wants.

Everyone, at all levels, should have opportunities for training, access to new positions, and participation in meetings, project teams, and the like. Management will be trained to ask and listen, as well as to tell and order. They should be trained to empower or delegate, to measure outcome, to involve subordinates in a bottom-up communication of recommendations for improvement, and to delegate to teams of peers. Leaders are expected to emerge from within the team.

A significant reward for excellence of input will be that the ideas get implemented. Publicize people at all hierarchical levels who initiated some new ideas, who took appropriate risks.

7

Moving Away From Fear—
Decrease Pressure

We have talked a lot about the disabling condition called Entitlement, but the opposite condition is just as debilitating. Fear, particularly at the extreme end of the curve where it becomes paralysis, destroys creative energy just as surely as the lethargy of Entitlement. Fear, anxiety, uncertainty mean the same thing: deep-down panic that your job is in jeopardy and the situation is out of your control.

To get back on track, organizations must first reduce anxiety by creating mechanisms by which people can earn reasonable levels of security. The parameters of what can be earned, the nature of the contract, and mutual expectations and requirements should be spelled out. People need to know what's being required and what they can expect.

Very simply, uncertainty is reduced when people are told what's going on and what will happen to them. In the vacuum of no news, employees imagine the worst. Since disappointment is much easier to handle than anxiety, honesty is the best policy.

The organization has to experience forward momentum, which requires that managers give employees short-term goals that are definitely and swiftly achievable, and executives create long-term wins. Employees need to know where they're heading, what's happening, and what strategies have been designed to get them there. As accomplishments are achieved, they must be loudly publicized and those who achieved them have to be visibly rewarded.

General Approaches

As with Entitlement, there are generalized strategies for each of the three Fear points on the Earning curve.

Point 9:	Support by addressing emotion.
Point 8:	Support through success and by addressing emotion.
Point 7:	Support through success.

The strategies take a slightly different focus on the organizational level than on the individual level (see sidebars).

When designing an intervention strategy it's important to assess how the state of Fear emerged. Was it a sudden shift caused by external forces (a hostile takeover)? Or was it a deliberate push away from years of Entitlement? We need to remember that where there's been a long period of Entitlement, anxiety has to be increased and maintained long enough for employees to believe it's a new ball game. Thus, if you're concerned with companies or individuals who are in the sector of Fear, especially in 7 or 8, because they've been forced out of Entitlement, then you must sustain pressure despite their discomfort with the high anxiety level. Only if they're at 9 should pressure be reduced.

On the other hand, if there's been a long period of very high anxiety, people need relief. It's conceivable that even more than experiences of success or triumph, they need a period of calm, in which things are stable and predictable and nothing much happens.

Organizations in Fear: What Leaders Must Do

Point 9. *Support by addressing emotion.* Executives need to project a sense that they know what is happening, they know how people feel, they care, and they want to help. Over and over, they need to communicate "It's better than it looks. We will be fine. It will be okay. In fact, it's going to be better than okay."

Point 8. *Support through success and by addressing emotion.* In this organization the major emphasis must be on the progress that surely is ahead as everyone works together. The message of progress must be simple and consistent: "We know it's been tough, but it's going to be better. More clearly than ever, we know what our real business is. Now we're in a much better position than ever to invest in our success. It will take time, but we're making it happen."

Point 7. *Support through success.* Emphasize the opportunities that lie in the future. Stress the organization's movements toward greater success and explain how individuals can contribute and participate it.

Individuals in Fear: What Managers Must Do

Point 9. *Support by addressing emotion.* People at 9 can't reduce anxiety through their own performance; the reassurance and support must be provided by others. Thus, managers need to be accessible and approachable. Let employees know that you understand how they are feeling. The message is "It's okay to feel the way you do. You're not alone in feeling that way. I am ready to help. It looks bad now, but it's really better than you think. And it's going to be a whole lot better. You're going to be fine."

Point 8. *Support through success and by addressing emotion.* People at 8 also need their emotional state to be acknowledged, but they need the anxiety-reducing experience of success as well. Maintain some amount of pressure, but keep the time frame short. Emphasize the idea that together, everyone will succeed. Recognize achievements, demonstrating that success is possible.

Managers could say "I know how you're feeling. It's hard right now, but if we pull together and work hard, it's going to be just fine. Here's exactly what to do. Get on the team. I know you're wondering what's going to happen, but it's going to get better, you'll see."

Point 7. *Support through success.* Provide goals (or require the individual to develop them) that involve opportunities to make decisions, learn new material, and meet some form of challenge. Success will breed confidence and confidence reduces anxiety. The attitude to communicate is "Here's a chance to show what you can do. I'm confident you can succeed."

In this chapter you will learn some specific strategies for adjusting the organizational temperature back toward the midrange of Earning. The strategies would work for all stages of Fear, but some are better for certain levels than others (check the numbers in parentheses in the list below). Once again, remember that seldom is an organization or an individual a perfect fit for any one level. Remember, too, that change has a way of twisting on you; the eventual outcome of your interventions may not exactly match your plan. In that case, take another assessment and start on a new course.

Here are suggested ways to lower anxiety levels:

Reducing Pressure: Nine Strategies

1. Make leadership visible (level 9).
2. Communicate concern for the individual (level 9).
3. Create trust in the organization (level 9).
4. Publicize achievements and restore confidence (level 8).
5. Provide information (level 8).
6. Make it possible for people to earn security and belonging (level 8).
7. Create procedures to enforce fairness (level 8).
8. Communicate goals and plans (level 8).
9. Reduce the emphasis on hierarchy (level 7).

Make Leadership Visible

When anxiety is high, so are dependency needs. Employees are looking to the leaders to give them faith that the future will be better. They are vulnerable and want to believe they can depend on those in command. That's why trust becomes especially important.

To maintain trust, leadership must be consistent. Credibility is lost when there are big discrepancies between what leaders say and what they do. In the wake of downsizing in the 1980s, there was a decrease in the perception that management practices what it preaches. Increasing credibility requires openness. Hidden agendas will destroy trust.

When uncertainty is high, leadership has to project certainty and confidence. People desperately need to believe that the leaders know what they are doing. Leaders must appear thoughtful, decisive, wise, and considerate. Management needs to increase its perceived trustworthiness, dedication, sagacity, and shrewdness.

Decisions sometimes must be made before you have all the information. It's what Barry Gibbons, CEO of Burger King, calls the theory of vacuum management. He says "When you make a major change, you create a kind of corporate vacuum while employees wait to see what happens. The trick is to fill that vacuum with positive ideas before others fill it with negative ones. This means telling people what's happening, what you're going to do."

Leadership must be very visible, both in person and through all the institutional media such as newsletters, magazines, and internal videotapes. Increase approachability; people want the sense that they can gain access to management. Practice management by walking around and encourage managers and top professionals to do the same. Get out of the office—literally. Be seen talking to people. Have lunch in the company cafeteria; stop and talk to people there. What you're doing is modeling approachability.

Use all opportunities to talk informally about what you plan to do, but don't be drawn into defensive arguing when employees complain. Especially if your organization is at 9, you'll need patience in dealing with behaviors that are unproductive and irritating but are hard to change: clinging to the past, rigidly hanging on to rules, denying changes in the organization's competitive position, and expressing contempt for management.

Communicate Concern for the Individual

In times of high anxiety, people want to feel that management cares about them personally and appreciates the efforts they're making. Employees need to believe that leadership understands how they feel and why, and is trying to help. Thus, leaders need to treat employees with as much kindness and generosity as possible.

Management needs to be especially thoughtful about communicating appreciation. Being personally thanked for your contribution is important at any time, but especially when stress is very high. Simultaneously, executives and managers need to acknowledge the high levels of uncertainty that are prevalent. That is, they need to thank employees for their loyalty and their work under difficult circumstances.

If the company is facing the need to restructure, demonstrate compassion for employees. Wherever possible, try to retain employees by retraining them or relocating them. If you do downsize, be as constructive as possible to those who must leave. As many forms of help as can be arranged should be offered and publicized, ranging from personal counseling to career counseling to financial advice.

Outplacement services are a way of acknowledging the recipient's contribution to the organization. For survivors of downsizing, stress is high and morale is low. Besides survivor guilt, employees worry about whether they'll be next. It's become clear that providing outplacement services is as useful to those who remain as those who are let go because survivors feel that it reflects the organization's conscience and concern.

Leadership needs to communicate an understanding of the stress that people are under and a commitment to help relieve it. Some form of attention akin to therapy may need to be made available to survivors, ranging from off-site individual or group counseling to group recreational activities.

If leadership is willing to act on the suggestions or complaints of employees, it should create mechanisms to gain that upward communication. Suggestions that will not be heard or taken should not be encouraged since they will only increase employees' sense of powerlessness and cynicism.

Create Trust in the Organization

In uncertain times, employees want to find strength in the institution. They want the sense that they are a part of something larger and stronger than themselves. They want to feel that it makes sense to commit to the organization because it will endure. Therefore, executives must emphasize and communicate the strength and endurance of the organization and its long-term commitment to maximizing the well-being of its members. They need to publicize the organization's history of overcoming problems and its legacy of breakthroughs.

While under terrible pressure to reduce uncertainty and generate the security of determined goals and rules, the executives must give the organization time to develop answers to the questions: "What is our business? What do we stand for?" The temptation for executives will be to latch on to some simple solutions that are currently chic. There are no simple solutions to complex issues. A new culture of values and goals and a set of procedures cannot be bought like a new suit. Consultants and academics can be used to facilitate or accelerate the rate of change, but developing a new culture takes time, because it must reflect the truth of what is important to that organization.

Trust is increased when leadership identifies and addresses any specific discrepancies between management statements and actions. During transitions there will be unavoidable discrepancies that need to be openly discussed.

Management must also be careful to minimize gestures that imply that the organization is shaky. When there's too much change and uncertainty, people attach a lot of importance to things that are, objectively speaking, minor. Be careful of little things that can become big symbols. People in one organization compiled a list of "take-aways," things that cost very little but that management had withdrawn in the period of crisis: Christmas parties, personalized notepads, spouses being invited to company functions, and magazine subscriptions. The removal of those inexpensive items broadcast "Woe is us!" more vividly than any headline in *The Wall Street Journal.* Those symbolic acts were the clincher and many employees left.

Publicize Achievements and Restore Confidence

In the face of high anxiety, people need a sense that the organization is successfully coping with something before they can tackle larger problems. Therefore, any increments of problem solving must be publicized and the people who accomplished goals must be heralded. Reward contributions visibly and significantly. Publicize progress and breakthroughs frequently and enthusiastically, including rewarding risk-taking attempts that have not yet shown success. Visibly praise the kinds of behavior or achievements that are desired such as making decisions, initiating changes, and thinking big.

Reinforce the message "You're such a select and outstanding group (or individual) that we expect you to succeed." Teach managers that employees typically perform at the levels expected of them.

It's much easier to achieve and gain confidence when the focus of efforts is external. Therefore, make efforts to focus energy on beating the competition; as much as possible, make it a game.

Provide Information

When they feel extremely anxious about their personal future, people are skeptical and critical. They'll be skeptical that they're being told the truth and critical of those who withhold it. Thus, the strategy has to be, good news or bad, tell the truth. People need to know what to expect. It is much easier to handle bad news than free-floating anxiety. Even bad news is better than no news. When their anxiety has been tempered, people can cope with bad news by problem solving.

When you tell the truth you increase people's sense of trust even if the news is bad. When anxiety is high and there's no real information, rumors multiply. And if people discover they've been lied to, rumors multiply even faster. Once the rumors start, they have a life cycle of their own. It becomes harder and harder to kill them.

In a period of high anxiety, very little appears logical and rational. Leadership must articulate why decisions were appropriate and how they will serve to improve conditions. The rational reasons for the changes need to be spelled out and communicated over and over. In fact, you have to overcommunicate, because when anxiety is high, people don't hear.

If the anxiety is high because of a change in focus or strategy, employees should be given the results of the changes, both negative (which they probably already know) and positive, as specifically as possible. If the changes had quantitative outcomes, provide numeric data. If the changes involved a broad perspective, such as a change in organizational philosophy, values, or culture, explain the justification for the changes. New policies have to be perceived as appropriate. Discontent, criticism, and a lack of faith or trust in leadership may be reduced by providing the rationale for change from the leaders' point of view.

Employees are better able to sustain high levels of anxiety if they feel confident that the period of turbulence is finite. If possible, tell people how long the transition and resulting turbulence are expected to take.

At the individual level, and for the same reasons, managers must tell the truth about how someone is regarded. In all manner of performance evaluations, managers must learn how to communicate the truth as they see it.

Because information is so important, managers need to know whether they're getting through. They may need to create mechanisms, such as internal questionnaires and surveys, to learn whether employees received and understood communications.

Make It Possible for People to Earn Security and Belonging

Employees have a right and a need to know what kind of job security they can earn, and what they have to do to earn it. It's all right to make security conditional, if the real contract is made overt and clear. People can handle the fact that they don't have absolute job security more easily than they can deal with the anxiety of not knowing what the contract really says.

- *Articulate your expectations.* Be clear about what is considered ideal behavior. Transmit that information in multiple ways, including training programs that cover risk taking, team behavior, creativity, and the like, especially for supervisors and managers. People who are models of those behaviors should be pointed out as examples.

Managers need to articulate the most important parts of employees' assignments so they know what to focus on. Ideally, descriptions of responsibilities are jointly developed by employees and their managers as a result of normal procedures, giving employees opportunities to have input into their assignments and ensuring that they're clear about what is expected.

- *Give everyone the chance to be a winner.* When the level of stress is already very high, it's a bad idea to increase competition. Under Fear conditions, techniques like forced ranking, where people are individually graded in comparison with others, or normalized distributions in which the number of A's or C's is determined by a bell-shaped curve, should not be used. Instead, leadership should create mechanisms by which everyone has the opportunity to succeed and win. IBM's 100 percent club is an example. While winning has to be earned by filling 100 percent of a quota, there are not limits on how many people can achieve or exceed their target.

- *Provide educational tools.* People need to be given the tools with which they can deal with issues and master their responsibilities. When changes in the marketplace engender change in the organization, and people feel their jobs are at risk, providing training in new skill areas is a very real lifeline and a very tangible way for companies to help reduce Fear. Also, when change is in the air, employees need help in becoming what the new organization will want.

Therefore, organizations need to create and encourage the use of educational opportunities related both to work and to personal growth. In addition to specific skill training, the organization must provide the education that will enable everyone to understand the reasons for change.

The computerization of work, in addition to other factors, is making workers obsolete at faster and faster rates. Job-related education subsidized by the organization is essential. It may be in the form of reimbursement of tuition at higher education institutions or it may include in-house workshops and classes.

Happily, many companies are making a serious investment in employee education. Business organizations have become the largest clients of two-year community and technical colleges around the country. Millions of production line workers are going to night school classes and almost two out of five workers under age thirty-five have some college training. A report by the Carnegie Foundation in 1985 found that between 80 and 90 percent of all U.S. corporations are offering tuition reimbursement, usually for job-related courses but sometimes for any class; some are even giving time off to go to school.

▪ *Avoid layoffs whenever possible.* If at all possible, when anxiety levels are very high, management should try to find alternatives to layoffs, especially with experienced people. Alternatives include exploring opportunities within the company; work-sharing where several employees work part-time; or lending an executive to a nonprofit institution like the Red Cross or a government agency on a shared salary basis.

▪ *Build a team environment.* In addition to some kind of job security (within reasonable parameters), people need to be able to earn the security of belonging, of being a member of the team or the family. Strive for an environment where interactions should be seen as cooperative and collaborative, not competitive. Life should not be seen as a zero-sum game where if one person wins another must lose. Instead, sharing resources and knowledge should be seen as a way by which everyone can increase their chances of success.

Encourage a sense of being a member of a team by diminishing competition within the group, by focusing energy outward to competitors, by creating mechanisms of identification as team members, and by rewarding team performance.

Create Procedures to Enforce Fairness

When anxiety is very high, people want the sense that they're protected from idiosyncratic behavior or prejudiced attitudes on the part of those who control what happens to them. They want the protection of fairness built into the system. That's clearest in terms of performance evaluations, compensation, and selection for promotion.

In many organizations, evaluation, selection, and pay are controlled by one person, an employee's boss. Under ordinary circumstances, that may be adequate. When anxiety levels are high, it's not. It doesn't create any sense of protection, of institutionalized equity.

That sense of fairness is best achieved when those decisions are made by a group of people who have clearly earned their position and the right to judge others. Also, the evaluation process should be one in which several judges are responsible for evaluating an employee. Each judge must state his or her opinion to the entire group. In that sense, within the group, evaluations are public. Also, the evaluators are themselves being evaluated by their peers. This shared, public process is especially valuable in evaluating work that is not quantifiable.

Communicate Goals and Plans

Leaders have to create the perception that they have some significant control over the present and the future of the organization because they know where the organization can and should go. In terrible circumstances, strategies for survival are adequate, but planning for victory is much more powerful.

Write a description of the values and culture of the organization in the future. Create a sense of that future by continuously communicating goals and the progress being made toward them. Create a sense of the individual's future by articulating the kinds of opportunities there will be in the future. If possible, tell people what the organization will be like and how their jobs will be affected. Cast it as something positive that people can work toward.

The emphasis should be on consistency of purpose and focus. Keep as long a time frame as possible in order to generate the perception of consistency. Goals, procedures, and rules should be kept as simple and flexible as possible so there's not much need for change, which adds to the perception of consistency. Decrease ambiguity, stress, and confusion.

Don't change the focus, goals, or strategy too often. You don't want people saying "Three years ago it was teamwork, next it was quality, then it was profit margins, and this year it's empowerment. I don't know what's really important anymore. I don't know on what basis I'm being judged."

Transform general goals into very concrete ones. Create specific targets, identify specific competitors, and create a concrete way of measuring performance. Provide unit or team goal statements, including "where we are, where we were, and where we're going now."

Regularly, let work units and individuals know how things are going. For work units or the organization as a whole, construct measurements of progress and broadcast the results. For individuals, institute measurements of achievement to reinforce people's experience that they're moving toward the target and to give them greater confidence that they will be able to succeed in the new conditions.

Goals or changes must be articulated simply, explicitly, and frequently. Every means of communication should be used with lots of examples. For instance:

> Our goal in shipping is to please our customer. We used to count how many containers went out the door. That didn't let us know whether or not the customer's needs were served. Now we're counting how many did or didn't arrive within the time we promised. We're counting how many did or didn't arrive in

excellent condition. If you look at the new forms you will see how we are measuring the quality of our deliveries. You will also see that each container now has a postcard stapled to the shipping label asking the customer to tell us how we did.

There is a hard balance here: Time must be given to develop goals and strategies while there has to be time pressure so people can't evade their responsibility to make decisions. With high anxiety, it's easy to evade decisions and commitments. As swiftly as possible, executives need to decide and then communicate what business are we in, what's our general strategy, what is each individual's piece, and what are the rules. People need to know exactly what they're supposed to do.

Reduce the Emphasis on Hierarchy

Anxiety is reduced when people have opportunities to earn greater confidence. They gain that confidence and a sense of having control over their lives when others are willing to acknowledge and respond to their knowledge, skill, competence, and experience whatever their formal status is. Thus, paradoxically, one of the best stratagems for easing stress is also one of the best for increasing it: Reduce the emphasis on hierarchy.

Employees at all levels need experiences of problem solving, decision making, and making a difference so they have some control over what's happening. Diminish the focus on pay grades. Don't permit descriptions like "He couldn't do that; he's a GS 5. We need a 7."

Give everyone opportunities to be a leader. The basic message has to be that despite tough times now, in the future there will be opportunities to be a winner. Teach people how to "grow their own job," or empower themselves. Leadership has to model empowerment through "handing-off" decision-making power. People have to know the limits of their autonomy or the parameters within which they are free to initiate and decide. Encourage risk taking by creating procedures by which managers "sign off" on a risky decision.

When people higher in nominal authority hand power to people lower down, by giving them the opportunity to initiate, to participate, and to decide, they are communicating respect for those people. Thus, in the long run, empowering people may be the most significant way to reduce anxiety.

We are entering an era of empowering employees. The role of manager and supervisor is changing from authority to facilitator. While the shift may require a lot of effort, the long-term benefits will include less passivity, a greater sense of personal power, more genuine teams that interact and stimulate creative performance, more honest interactions, and greater productivity.

8

Maintaining the Creative Energy of Earning

In the midsector of the curve—points 4, 5, and 6—organizations are in Earning, which means they are not in problem positions. Therefore, the focus is not so much on how to improve performance as it is on how to maintain current levels; not on how to move out of Entitlement or Fear but how to avoid moving out of Earning.

The three overall strategies, one for each point in the Earning sector of the Earning curve, are as follows:

Point 4:	Encourage risk taking.
Point 5:	Focus on sustaining excellence.
Point 6:	Encourage prudence.

And here, too, the strategies take slightly different forms depending on whether they are applied to organizations or to individuals.

For Organizations—What Executives Must Do

Point 4. *Encourage risk-taking.* This organization is productive and basically admirable, but it lacks the excitement of enjoying a higher level of risk. It is characterized more by

prudence than by exhilaration. It's desirable to move this organization into 6 occasionally because a big win can excite
the whole organization as well as those who specifically par-
ticipated.

The basic message for leaders to communicate throughout the organization is "Don't try to get consensus so quickly;
it creates too many compromises from the start of decision
making. We need a leadership style that encourages thinking
big, at least some of the time. Let's create a fund for innovative pilot projects. Let's go for a breakthrough!"

To stimulate risk taking, the organization must work
toward creating small pockets of entrepreneurial activity, of
"skunkworks." This may require hiring innovative leaders
from outside, renting separate space, or allowing unique procedures and an autonomous budget. While suggestions for
risky projects can come from the organization's executives,
it's better to open the process to the organization as a whole.

Innovations and innovators should be widely publicized.
Even if the project is only partially successful, it should be
visible because it's a model of what the organization wants to
increase. While most work will involve teams, rewards should
go to individuals as well as to teams.

A good example to follow is 3M Corporation. Create the
assumption that every year 15 to 20 percent of your products
will be new and make rewards dependent on meeting that
goal. The culture can say "We assume continuous improvement, but we reserve the largest rewards for breakthroughs."

The organization will train people in creative confrontation or healthy disagreement. Instead of focusing on amicable
consensus, there needs to be agreement that divergent thinking provides creative potential. At 4, the organization's publicized goal should be "No more marching penguins."

Point 5. *Focus on sustaining excellence.* Without stress
or crisis it's difficult to sustain maximum involvement and
motivation. The leaders of the organization should be thinking "We have to be careful. We're in the most dangerous of
conditions—we're doing great. It's very easy now to believe
our own publicity and think we're perfect. Now's the time to

really watch the competition. We're about to install assess-ment of all our operating units. Stay sharp!''

This organization will require change for its own sake. Goals must be continuously raised so the challenge is harder. Every so often, the structure is organized to create realign-ments, so that relationships change. Lateral transfers to dif-ferent functions or kinds of responsibilities are a normal part of everyone's career.

Organizations at point 5 need to create an ongoing sense of competition with other companies, especially if they're large and powerful. Also, the organizations may profit from periodic reviews by impartial, knowledgeable outsiders.

This organization assumes continuous education. In ad-dition to paying tuition, some people are sent, on the basis of competitive merit, to pursue degrees while on salary. This or-ganization invests in people's creativity as well as knowledge as people earn sabbaticals. This organization requires a cul-ture that presumes excellence.

Point 6. *Encourage prudence.* Often what we call inno-vation is not so much a gigantic breakthrough as an accu-mulation of small, incremental changes. In fact, as Michael Porter writes in the *Harvard Business Review,* "It often in-volves ideas that are not even 'new'—ideas that have been around, but never vigorously pursued."

Organizations that are at 6 do not give much attention to incremental modifications or progress. Applause is reserved for big breakthroughs. As a result, many smaller opportuni-ties for improvement can be ignored. These organizations need to collect data within their own units, or within their competitors', demonstrating the cumulative effect of small gains, which can become very significant. There must be a factual demonstration that small gains are also a significant opportunity.

There's also the possibility that the pursuit of the big one threatens appropriate prudence. This organization needs pro-cedures that impose some caution, procedures that slow the process slightly and require thoughtful consideration of alter-natives, especially potential negative outcomes.

These procedures could involve, for example, reviews by special committees or a requirement that proposed decisions be formally defended before they are implemented. They could also involve training in formal techniques of problem solving, which could become a required style of making decisions. In this way the organization uses structure or rules of procedure to impose limits on impulsivity.

Organizations can be at 6 naturally, because they're entrepreneurial and they enjoy risk. They can also be at 6 (instead of 5) because management continuously exerts too much pressure for performance, with the result that people never quite gain any sense that they've earned security. That kind of pressure can be exerted vertically from the top down and also laterally by peers.

This organization needs to lighten up. Pressures that are not being created out of the reality of competition or other work conditions should be lessened, including not making fine distinctions between performers. Limit the number of performance categories to a few; then the great majority of employees will be evaluated as "very good," and very few will be judged as "outstanding" or "unsatisfactory."

The criteria of performance must be high, but there should be no limit on how many people are permitted to succeed. Don't use one-on-one competition or ranking with this population because then every winner makes other people losers. While employees may be able to earn bonuses, no part of their salary should be at risk. As almost everyone performs very well, there should be few distinctions between them in the rewards they can and do earn.

For Individuals—What Managers Must Do

Point 4. *Encourage risk taking.* For individuals who seem to be at point 4, continually encourage them to stretch. They should be hearing this message from their managers: "I know it's a nice feeling to be a member of the team, but every time you have a big idea and the others don't cheer right away, you seem to back off. Remember, breakthrough ideas mean you're either coming out of left field or you're way ahead of the pack. Give the others time to catch up with you. Don't give up so easily."

Point 5. *Focus on sustaining excellence.* Position 5 is the ideal state. People who've reached 5 tend to stay there, as being a 5 comes to be a critical part of their self-esteem. Managers can nourish and maintain this state by communicating this basic message: "You are terrific and I want you to know how much we appreciate your contributions. You are an outstanding performer in an excellent team. Do you have any ideas that I haven't heard about for improving your own or your group's performance even more?"

Point 6. *Encourage prudence.* Managers might say "I really admire your innovativeness. You're ready to take on challenges that would scare most people. But sometimes I think your follow-through isn't as good as it could be. A lot of improvements come from making the details better. Think about finding a partner who likes to do that kind of work."

Make Yourself the Model

When you are trying to optimize performance, your basic strategy is to encourage 4's to take bigger risks and to ease 6's toward greater prudence. One way is to be a model of what you want to see. To encourage others toward greater risk taking, you could publicly show your willingness to take on longer projects or initiate more substantial change than usual. To demonstrate prudence, you could make decisions based largely on precedent, and make sure people know that's your basis. Depending on the need, you can pay attention to or ignore the guidelines of custom; you can challenge or support the cultural assumptions.

In a more directive strategy, managers can require that subordinates analyze assumptions and determine whether they're still appropriate. They can require changes in the styles of how decisions are made, pushing their people toward either more risk or a bit more caution. They can designate individuals who use the preferred style as a formal leader.

The more important issue is for management not to behave in ways that demotivate this group. This population consists of people who are sufficiently excellent that management must be careful not to burden them with work that isn't important. Because they're likely to be experts, which is an advantage for management, managers may tend to keep these people doing the same work for longer than is optimal for the employee. Management must create opportunities for new responsibilities, risk, and learning.

With these excellent performers, don't tell; instead, consult, collaborate, and participate. Assume excellence and verbalize that assumption.

Creating the Conditions of Earning

To get commitment and high performance, organizations need to create the conditions that will give people opportunities to be winners. Companies at points 4, 5, and 6 need most of all to nurture the creative energy that is already buzzing throughout the place. Imagine all employees were volunteers. What would motivate them to come to work?

> "What I'm doing is significant. It makes a difference. *I* make a difference."
>
> "What I'm doing is important and it has an impact on something I care about."
>
> "I really care about this stuff and I'm one of the people who's making it happen."
>
> "I'm really challenged. I keep on growing and the leash is long."
>
> "My ideas are respected. I have a lot of say in what gets done and how it's done."
>
> "It's fun! It's a great group of people and we're in it together. We're winning!"

Where people have those kinds of attitudes toward their work, you have an environment of Earning.

Do those statements sound familiar? Think back to the section in Chapter 4 that described the three conditions that motivate people, that give them a sense of job enrichment:

1. Challenge
2. Empowerment
3. Significance

Remember that we discovered these are the same conditions that nurture productivity and innovation? Thus, we can say that the task of maintaining a climate where Earning can thrive is the task of converting those three psychological needs into management actions.

Challenge

Challenge is the opportunity to learn or master something new. It inevitably means risk, since people who try something new can never be certain they'll succeed. Risk is a vital part of the experience of challenge and is the core of the sense of having fun at work. When people say they want challenge, they're saying they want to learn, to do different work, and to push to the edge of their comfort zone.

I often ask people "What have you ever done that gave you a special sense of accomplishment?" In answer, they almost never refer to something that got them a reward of some kind. Instead, they remember the times when they stood up to risk and succeeded. They say things like:

> "I was required to get technical training, which I would never have done, and when I was finished I wrote a paper and it got published."
> "I created a training program against lots of opposition and it was terrific."
> "I went into work where there were no other women."
> "I made the presentation of our project, and it was to people who were all senior to me."

"I had to negotiate some tricky clauses with the union and
I did it and we all felt like we'd won."

"I was asked to do a special assignment that involved auto-
mating our compensation system and I hadn't had any
computer experience up to then."

As people meet this kind of challenge, they learn a lot:

"It was an exciting time."

"I learned to really delegate."

"I found people loved being part of the team."

"I found everybody has more ability than they ever knew,
and that includes me."

Require the Stretch

Organizations can always create opportunities for people
to be challenged. The key is to raise your expectations. High
expectations are terrific motivators. When little is expected, little is given. In organizations with a psychology of Earning, the
basic assumption is that everyone is capable of achieving and
succeeding. The culture of the organization will take that for
granted. People generally perform at the level they are expected to perform.

Tolerate Mistakes

Another thing we must do, if we genuinely want to stimulate challenge, is learn to tolerate mistakes. A culture of Earning must include the sense that it's okay to make some mistakes
because that will happen with innovation and learning, especially when the challenge is complex. Although no organization
can tell employees to simply plow ahead and not to worry about
making errors, there has to be an attitude that reasonable and
occasional mistakes are opportunities to learn something.

In August 1990, Pacific Bell's top leadership held a day-
long meeting to introduce to middle managers a new organizational structure that PacBell believes will permit greater focus
on customers and markets. Following the presentation, the
team answered questions from the audience.

QUESTION FROM AN EMPLOYEE: Often, people learn best by failing. Are you willing to tolerate failure? Do you think it is required?

BOB LEE *(executive vice-president, statewide markets):* Clearly we're moving into an environment where we have to accept risk. I have a pen that says "Eight out of ten is better than three out of three." In the past, we've been a business that aimed for—and got—three out of three, and it took us a long time to do that. We have to become the kind of company that shoots for—and gets—eight out of ten.

PHIL QUIGLEY *(president and CEO):* One of my mentors was the man who invented the Mickey Mouse telephone—he literally broke the telephone barrier with respect to product. I asked him once when we were flying together what the difference was between the corporate type and the entrepreneurial type. He said the corporate type has all the resources and all the time to make a decision—and they make those decisions right 98 percent of the time. The entrepreneurial type probably makes the right decision six out of ten times—but they're the decisions that really make an impact.

Promote Self-Challenge

While organizations, in the form of managers, can give people developmental or challenge experiences, it's very important that individuals themselves realize there are always opportunities for learning, if they'll look for them. People who work in large organizations especially are prone to wait for the organization to create the experience. Instead, people ought to be held responsible for finding and initiating these opportunities for themselves, because that can result in a greater sense of personal power and confidence than stepping up to an assignment they did nothing to generate.

In that kind of environment, continuously moving into what's new or meeting a challenge will be taken for granted, because that's the usual thing people do. Change will be at the core of ordinary routine. People will look for chances to contribute to the mainstream and improve the business where it counts.

If the circumstances are really good, there'll be ways for everyone to compete and win, and so competitive hostility will be directed outward, to the institution's competition. That's exactly what's happening in Industrial Computer Source, the company we visited in the beginning of Chapter 4.

Empowerment

Empowerment means sharing power, increasing autonomy, throughout the organization. It means giving everyone—instead of just people with certain positions or certain job titles—the legitimate right to make judgments, form conclusions, reach decisions, and then act. The point is not to spread power around willy-nilly but to pinpoint it, to move the decision as close as possible to the point where action can be taken: on the production line, on the shop floor, in the back office, in the functional departments.

Respect the Many Forms of Achievement

The process of empowerment is based on the recognition that good ideas can come from anywhere, that achievement takes many forms and all of them deserve respect. Coping with change is the major impetus for listening to anyone, at any grade, who has something to offer. That's why empowerment is a required management style when things are different or unpredictable. Familiarity with or a mastery of what happened before isn't always the best guide for what should be done now, when there's a lot of change. When the risks are high and so are the unknowns, it's necessary to pull together as a team. When you have to master the unknown, you're more prone to listen to whoever learns the fastest or knows the most, wherever they are on the ladder.

I learned that in an unexpected way with two of my children. When they were adolescents, aged fifteen and sixteen, our family set out on a year-long trip wandering around Central and South America. We, their parents, had not anticipated how irrelevant our professional skills would be. What we did at home that gave us formal power—being professors of nuclear physics and psychology—were not exactly critical skills when we were trying to buy fruit and vegetables from Native Americans in their outdoor market.

It turned out that the sixteen-year-old was the world's second best navigator, the first being Magellan. Unflappable, she'd sit in the copilot's seat and direct the driver through urban sprawl or mountain crags. She also turned out to be really talented in language, and within two months she could manage in Spanish. The fifteen-year-old was a good car mechanic when we started out. Six months into the trip, he'd become an excellent mechanic. He was also a hotshot at bargaining, an integral part of life in that culture.

Under ordinary circumstances, American adolescents are tolerated by their parents who are praying they won't get into trouble and waiting for them to grow up. In the usual conditions, our teenagers don't have skills or knowledge that allow them to earn the respect of adults as peers. On that trip, the two kids had skills we needed; they were better in some necessary things than their parents. As they did those things, they earned our respect. While they were always our children, they also became our peers much of the time.

Diminish the Hierarchy

In an empowering organization there's a generalized assumption that everybody is competent, if not yet, then after they've had a chance to learn. People in these organizations have developed the belief that what they accomplish is at least as important as their formal status or rank in the hierarchy. They believe that real contributions earn them the right to influence others. In other words, empowering organizations will give different kinds of people opportunities to lead. Thus, empowering organizations will have several kinds of leadership derived from different kinds of power.

Another thing we must do to create the conditions where Earning can flourish is rid ourselves of the caste system mentality that goes with a rigid hierarchy. We must begin to see workers at all levels as assets, not problems to be managed by a few decision makers at the top.

A caste system is dispiriting and demotivating because no matter how well you work or how much you know, until you get on the higher rungs of the ladder you can't get recognized as a significant player. Of course, that leads to a lack of involvement and, in the long run, a disinterest in working toward common goals for the good of the organization.

Shaking off this caste way of thinking will not be easy. U.S. industry has operated in a hierarchical mode for many years, starting with the "efficient" operations of auto makers in the early twentieth century, where a few at the top made decisions for the many on the assembly lines and those at the bottom were expected to do what they were told. But now, in the reality of worldwide competition, American institutions are painfully learning the cost of this legacy of not involving employees at all levels in continual problem solving. A psychologically hierarchical organization loses input from subordinates at all levels, including professionals and management.

New Management Attitudes

Empowered people are supposed to think and evaluate; input is expected from everyone. In a practical sense, that means managers do a lot of listening. Those higher up in the hierarchy make sure they hear those who are lower down.

If people are to be empowered, management has to believe that the person who does the work knows more about it than anyone else and is therefore the best one to improve how it is done. Deep down, many managers still believe they have more experience than workers. They may be willing to listen, but they are rarely willing to let lower-level people—the ones actually doing the work—make the decisions.

We need to set up what Robert Waterman calls "directed autonomy." This idea simply means there are boundaries as well as freedoms: People have to know what their boundaries are. They need to know when they can act on their own and when they should consult with their boss. The boss has to establish the boundaries and decide when to require consultation and when to get out of the way. Managers create the space within which people can be autonomous, and outside of which there are limits to their freedom to act. In a good organization, one where people are required to be responsible for themselves, the individual and the organization will collaborate in ways that make the space larger and larger. It's another way to think about what empowerment involves.

It may require a mind-set shift. Managers have to give up attitudes of superiority. They have to stop thinking "I have to tell them what to do and how to do it." They have to give up the idea that "If I'm not watching and judging, they'll do a lousy job." Giving up this authoritarian view has a direct payback: the end of adversarial relations.

New Employee Attitudes

Jack Welch, the dynamic CEO of General Electric, describes the ideal manager-employee relationship:

> Ultimately, we're talking about redefining the relationship between the boss and the subordinate. I want to get to a point where people challenge their bosses every day: "Why do you require me to do these wasteful things? Why don't you let me do the things you shouldn't be doing so you can move on and create? That's the job of a leader—to create, not to control. Trust me to do my job, and don't make me waste all my time trying to deal with you on the control issue."
>
> [People] will develop the personal courage to speak out. The norm will become the person who says, "Dammit, we're not doing it. Let's get on with doing it." . . . This process will create more fulfilling and rewarding jobs. The quality of work life will improve dramatically.

New Leader Attitudes

It's fashionable to talk about empowerment right now, and some of what is said is too sweet. Empowering organizations are not led by Ms. or Mr. Pollyanna. I've always found that the leaders in those organizations became leaders because they're among the smartest of a group of really smart people. And they're very comfortable being judgmental. They have earned their position of authority and are very outspoken. But they don't need to embellish their power, so they use the word *participatory* a lot. They say their job is to set a strategic direction and get people to buy into it, to give others money and authority, and then to leave them alone to do the work. In discussions they listen a lot as they also prod and challenge.

Reuben Mark, CEO of Colgate-Palmolive, is one such leader. He says "The more [power] you have, the less you should use. You consolidate and build power by empowering others. I don't like to talk about power. I prefer to think of it as responsibility and authority."

Ralph Stayer, CEO of Johnsonville Foods, said "Real power is getting people committed. Real power comes from giving it up to others who are in a better position to do things than you are." And he puts his words into action. Since 1985 people from Johnsonville's shop floor have written the manufacturing budget; they volunteer for the task. Another group of volunteers designs the manufacturing line. If the workers want new equipment, they work up the cash flow analysis.

Stayer's approach is to establish a climate in which goals are set as far down in the company as possible; top managers then spend their time choosing which goals should have first claim on the company's capital. In 1988, for instance, the sales department set a goal of increasing sales volume by 40 percent, and the manufacturing group backed them up by setting their own goal of providing the additional output while holding cost increases to 20 percent.

Since 1983, Johnsonville has doubled its return on assets, and sales have increased more than 15 percent a year—twice as fast as the payroll.

Significance

Most of us need to feel that our work matters: "It matters that I do it and it's important enough that it better be done well.

I have to take my work seriously because there are important consequences if it's done well or badly. What I do now will have an impact on me and this organization (or occupation) in the future. I'm not wasting my time going through the motions. This is important and I take it seriously."

In contrast, people don't feel their work is significant if the following is true:

- It's not obviously connected to what that organization's business is.
- It doesn't result in something that can be measured in terms of outcome or impact.
- It's work that fulfills bureaucratic requirements and involves shuffling papers and/or going to endless meetings.

Researchers Lorsch and Takagi found that people remained exceptionally committed to their work when their job involved responsibilities that contributed to the company. When their performance had an impact on the organization's results, they felt significant. When their efforts led to success for the organization, they felt like winners. In short, they had the sense that they counted and they had an impact on the present and the future of the organization. And the organization was important to them, so it was important that they do their work well.

Organizations have tried to help people feel their work is significant by showing them how it ultimately contributes to the company. Of course, that helps, but it's not the most effective thing they can do. More important, I think, is to do the work of figuring out how each person can contribute to what the business really does.

All employees with their supervisors should think through these questions:

- What is my function?
- What do I contribute?
- How do I make a difference?

Then management should allow people to increase those significant aspects of their job and reduce or eliminate as much as possible of the rest.

It's a good idea for supervisors and managers to routinely ask people if they think their work contributes and ask how they think they might contribute more. It's conceivable that people have very different opinions about what is significant.

One of the best things companies can do for people who are not in the mainstream of the business is to assign them to temporary committees or task forces that are engaged in significant projects. I once asked a person in a major computer manufacturing company what her job was. She was embarrassed. In a company known for state-of-the-art product development, her job was to keep the organizational chart current. As people changed their job, she changed the chart in the mainframe computer. The work, we might argue, was necessary, but it wasn't significant. She needed an opportunity to feel that she made a real difference.

If I were her manager I'd ask her to look around and find activities, programs, committees, and task forces that she'd like to do as part of her job. If she didn't find any, I'd made a few suggestions. (In theory I guess we might also try to find someone who thought keeping the chart current was an important thing to do.)

In an article about how Korea won the microwave war, Ira Magaziner and Mark Patinkin describe a worker named Hwang. Her job is to attach the serial numbers and name-brand labels to Samsung microwave ovens. She attaches about 1,200 labels a day. Six days a week, hour after hour, she does the same simple thing. Even after the inspector has double-checked her work, she herself checks it one more time.

She says her job is a challenge to her personal discipline, thus to her integrity. "I put my spirit, my soul, in this product." If you do it perfectly every time, she says, you are teaching yourself excellence. And Hwang remembers it wasn't so long ago that Korea was poor. It's not poor anymore. Hwang believes that she is contributing to something very important—to Korea itself. On many levels, this mundane task is significant to her.

Doing work that is significant also can mean finding opportunity for personal expression in a job. We want to feel that what we do is enduring. That purpose provides the motive toward excellence. It's not about money. It's about our psychological need to feel that our work expands the purpose and meaning of our life; money is just a way of keeping score.

Not long ago, billionaire Warren Buffett visited the Nebraska Furniture Mart that his company, Berkshire Hathaway, had acquired. He spent the day with Mrs. Rose Blumkin, who established the store fifty years ago with $500. Today the store is the largest of its kind and Mrs. Blumkin is ninety-four years old. She's at work seven days a week. She gets around in an electric golf cart and says she's having a ball.

Neither Mr. Buffett nor Mrs. Blumkin needs money. Buffett says "Money is a by-product of something I like to do very much. Every day, when I get to the office, so to speak, I do a little tap dance."

9

The New Paradigm

Since the mid-1970s, we have tumbled from our perch of economic dominance. Although it hurts, the fall has the potential of galvanizing us to new ways of thinking and working that will serve us far better in the 1990s. Indeed that's what happened. For a discussion of the constructive outcome of America's economic crisis of the 1980s, see Chapter 16.

The 1980s began with the deepest postwar recession we ever had. We had double-digit inflation and interest rates. OPEC tried to strangle the economy. Many manufacturers struggled to survive and many didn't. Our budget deficit and our trade deficit were alarming. Competition increased on all sides at a frightening rate, and old-line companies, long dominant in their industry, found themselves uncompetitive.

Yet Americans seem to be driven by crisis. During the 1980s, as things got worse, many things got better. Many U.S. manufacturers got lean and aggressive. Many reorganized. Some of the changes were wrenching: firings, voluntary early retirements, leveraged buyouts, mergers, and acquisitions.

The result is that we've become competitive in many sectors of industry. Many who found themselves losing in international competition have learned to create quality and value. Our economy created an incredible number of new jobs. Though huge, our deficits are now a smaller percentage of our economy than they were.

Despite all the gloom, our economy is stronger than pessimists contend and our standard of living remains the highest in the world. Using purchasing power parities (a measure of what the same amount of money would buy in another country), the Bureau of Labor Statistics has calculated that in 1988 West Germany's purchase value was 72 percent of U.S. levels and Japan's was 81 percent.

On the other hand, we still have large sectors of the economy within which Entitlement flourishes. And, when I look at survivors within those organizations that downsized, reorganized, merged, and fired, I fear we are again in danger of decline. During downsizing or after the merger or buyout, there's a lot of fear. Because the downsizing is a necessary response to a loss of market share or a decrease in tax revenues, people usually respond with increased efforts to make things better. As long as the anxiety is not paralyzingly high, productivity rises.

But when the crisis is over, so is the sense of alarm.

In organizations where Entitlement prevailed, what I see after the crisis seems to pass is the reinstatement of Entitlement. When the worst seems over, a reality of no risk is recreated. This situation, I believe, is what happened at Kodak.

The Kodak Experience

In 1983, Colby Chandler became chairman and chief executive officer of the century-old company that one analyst has called a "bureaucratic behemoth." Almost immediately, the company laid off thousands of workers, for the first time in corporate history. I was there, and it was surrealistic. People continued to go to meetings and chat, and no one said anything about the layoffs.

The next year, profits were up by 63 percent, and then started to slip; a second restructuring was announced. Through 1985 and part of 1986, the company had six straight quarters of losses. Another restructuring took place: 10,000 more people were laid off and a cost-cutting program was set up. Profits more than tripled the following year, and set a record in 1988, when net profit increased 60 percent over 1985, and net earnings were up by 322 percent. Then, in 1989, profits fell by 23 percent in the first quarter, and the company announced cost-cutting plans that included more layoffs. All in all, the company went through four separate restructurings in seven years, eliminating some 25,000 employees, including managers. In that time, long-term debt increased from less than 5 percent of total capital to more than 46 percent.

What was happening? There was increased competition, a periodic rise in the value of the dollar, and high expenses associated with the 1988 acquisition of Sterling Drug Company. But it is also plausible that Kodak, which enjoyed unequalled Entitlement for more than a century, keeps reverting back to it as soon as the pressure of a crisis passes. One stock analyst observing the period of ups and downs commented in mid-1989 that "It seems like they wipe their brow and say, 'Whew, we're glad that's over,' and then they turn around and have to do it all over again."

A related factor, of course, is the leadership of Kodak. Chandler, who at first seemed determined to breathe life into the "behemoth," made changes that most observers consider too slow and too gentle. In mid-1989, after those seven years of reorganizations, analysts still characterized Kodak as a benevolent corporate father and Chandler as a paternalistic caretaker. "Their idea of dramatic cost-cutting and dramatic restructuring isn't that dramatic. They still have a mentality that is somewhat paternalistic."

And where are they now? In June 1989, the "tough-talking" Kay Whitmore took over as chairman and CEO. Late that year, he put in place yet another restructuring, cutting 4,500 workers and linking managers' compensation directly to corporate profits.

Alas, it wasn't enough. Kay Whitmore may have talked tough, but he learned his management style in the Entitled culture of Kodak. Mr. Whitmore was hampered because he took Kodak's torturous style of doing business for granted. Eastman Kodak's board replaced him in October 1993 with George Fisher, the CEO of the very successful Motorola.

New Leadership Style for a New Era

Shaking out of Entitlement is a profound change, and it must be accompanied by changes in management style. Increasingly, today's strategies for creating change reflect the paradigm shift toward empowerment. Today's progressive leaders need to know how to get people to work as collaborative teams, and that is a very different skill from what managers were expected to possess fifteen years ago.

Management's task, therefore, is increasingly one of setting direction and then motivating and harnessing the collective and creative energies of everyone involved. Ralph Stayer, CEO of Johnsonville Foods, describes this change in terms of power, which of course is exactly what it is:

> Before, I didn't have power because I had people wandering around not giving a damn. Real power is getting people committed. Real power comes from giving it up to others who are in a better position to do things than you are. Control is an illusion. The only control you can possibly have comes when people are controlling themselves.

The new style of managing is based on the idea that other people may know more about something than you do, even though your status is higher. At IBM, for example, when an engineer gets stuck on a problem it may be entered into the computer and ideas may be received from 70,000 people. Simultaneously, the entire organization can work on a problem.

Solving the problems, moving toward the goals, is increasingly the task of teams of workers who come together in shifting combinations. As William Taylor wrote, "Corporate cultures have to move toward a philosophy of shared problems and challenges—task forces that arise from the mist, attack a problem, and then go away."

In the new paradigm, managers and supervisors who are accustomed to being in control are now being asked to give that control over to the people they manage. Many find this task difficult. It is common to find a lot of confusion and high levels of anxiety among supervisors and managers in organizations shifting from the old paradigm to the new. Some will not be able to make the transition and will have to be replaced. But even those who successfully change may continue to experience more uncertainty about their role than is optimal.

Therefore, supervisors and managers need a considerable period of strong support. That support must come first from the executive level. The organization's leadership must provide statements about style and values, must create and fund strong management development programs, and must create opportunities for supervisors and managers to meet and discuss issues relevant to them. It's also helpful if support, in the form of nonadversarial behavior, comes from the employees as well. This tends to happen naturally when employees share the values and are given opportunities to learn about and offer input for changes.

The New Employment Contract

The old employment contract, founded in the psychology of Entitlement, promised almost absolute job security. The new contract, founded on Earning, promises job security of a different sort. The criteria for success and for belonging will rest on achievement.

The new contract says "If you are productive and add value, if you keep on learning and your skills are current, you'll be okay. In fact, our half of the bargain is to keep creating opportunities for you to achieve. Your half of the bargain is to keep on achieving."

For the employees' part, people feel more secure when the organization's basic attitude is that people who work there are competent, honest, and intelligent. That implies the organization will not be tricky in how it deals with people. And those feelings of security are increased when the organization makes commitments to its employees as part of its formal corporate values, like IBM's "Respect for the Individual" (see sidebar).

IBM's Guiding Principles: Respect for the Individual

Our basic belief is respect for the individual, for each person's rights and dignity. It follows from this principle that IBM should:

> a. Help employees develop their potential and make the best use of their abilities.
> b. Pay and promote on merit.
> c. Maintain two-way communications between manager and employee, with opportunity for a fair hearing and equitable settlement of disagreements.

Another aspect of security is knowing that the company will be straight with you. People feel more secure when they know the truth about where they stand and how their organization is doing. Trust that comes from long-term honest communication is an important factor in the psychology of Earning. Organizations do better when they don't clobber people, but they also don't evade the hard issues.

Another part of the new contract is a mutual understanding that people's performance on the job—and nothing else—determines their success or failure. Evaluation procedures must protect people from prejudiced and idiosyncratic behavior on the part of superiors. Furthermore, this performance/rewards balance must be genuine. Unless there is a direct relationship between levels of performance directed to specific outcomes and what happens to people, all you have is empty talk.

We know that people respond to what they're held accountable for. If companies tell employees to "pay attention to your customer" but actually measure the amount of product that is shipped out the door, then good customer service doesn't really count.

To get employees to pay attention to the customer, you must hold them specifically accountable for customer service. The evaluation of their performance has to be tied directly to the goal of satisfying the customer. If they add to customer satisfaction, they should be rewarded. If they don't increase customer satisfaction, some penalty must occur. Slogans by themselves are irrelevant.

It is increasingly clear that employees are capable of doing excellent work and will do it when excellence is expected and when they understand why excellence is important. The new contract, in summary, defines the new kind of organization we need to be working toward. In the new paradigm:

- People at all levels are given the opportunity to show what they can do. There are lots of leaders.
- Most work is done in small teams of peers, led by people who are knowledgeable in the particular area of concern.
- People are given continuous challenges, along with support.
- Managers are coaches, not dictators.
- Ability and contribution count more than status.
- Rewards reflect real contribution.
- Accountability is enthusiastically embraced, as people see a direct payoff.

The Dynamics of Change

A reversal of values is a huge change. Those who are trying to make it happen need to have a clear vision of what they want to accomplish; they need to measure progress and broadcast those results to everyone, and they must have patience.

They need patience because major change takes a long time. Jack Bowsher found it took smaller organizations five years to implement a fundamental change in just their educational system, and large organizations take eight to ten. Unless a crisis threatens, making the need for changes inescapably obvious, a change to Earning, to empowerment, and to accountable will take at least that long.

It's easy to lose sight of the real problem. When organizations don't keep that in the center of their vision, their solutions go not to the core where the real issue is but instead to the periphery. Then attention is directed to creating a mission statement or teaching team building. While those peripheral solutions may be important and constructive, addressing them is not sufficiently motivating. Only when there's a sense of danger do you get real energy and long-term commitment to deal with the pain and anxiety of change.

Therefore, to get fundamental change on an organization-wide basis, find either (1) a part of the organization that is in real trouble—danger looms if it doesn't change, so there is a real reason for the change—or (2) a part of the organization that has had a real problem, made changes, and thus had the experience of converting the problem into an opportunity.

Many well-intentioned change programs fail because there is a lack of understanding of how the change process works. Organizations assume that the place to start is with the individual: Get individuals to change and automatically the organization changes too. This belief is exactly backward. Behavior of employees, as individuals, is powerfully affected by their role in the organization. Therefore, the most direct route to change is to give people a new role.

That's what my recommendations concerning increasing or decreasing people's sense of risk are intended to do. I'm not suggesting that you try and talk people into changing how they behave (although I do recommend explaining what you are doing and why). Rather, I'm describing ways in which organizations can alter the conditions of work. I'm describing ways companies can create change in the conditions of people's experience. Then, because there are negative or positive consequences to what people do, behavior changes. And then, attitudes will change too.

Personally, I don't believe people change in response to concepts or abstractions. They change because they need to, because they feel there's a real danger if they don't change. Leaders can encourage and foster change, but in the end it rests on the shoulders of the employees who will be affected.

The New Paradigm Taking Shape at Ford

It's hard to imagine a company more American than Ford Motor Company. For years, Ford products have symbolized American enterprise. Ford was so solid that it forgot about the customer. When the economic picture began to change in the 1970s, no one in Detroit was paying attention.

Lee Miskowski is a vice-president and general manager of the Parts and Service Division. In an eloquent and dramatic speech delivered in 1987, he describes the trouble that began in the late 1970s—economic recession, oil embargoes, and frightening competition from Japan—that "changed forever the environment in which we do business."*

The effect on Ford was catastrophic: three straight years of billion-dollar losses. Miskowski says "We lost more money in those three years than we made in the first eighty years of our corporate history." At first there was nothing but a kind of corporate disbelief. Another Ford executive describes the reaction:

> The first year the loss was a total surprise. We had no idea things were that bad. No one imagined we'd do it a second time. The third year we were absolutely amazed. There was a lot of denial, but we got the message: Something was terribly, fundamentally wrong.

Ford demonstrated the truth we have learned: If things are bad enough, change is possible, even in the most entrenched bureaucracies. Miskowski explains:

> For the first time, I think, we came down from our ivory towers. We were literally shocked into understanding that we had become comfortable with some inefficient, outdated ways of thinking and working that simply had to be replaced.

Both Ford executives I talked with agreed that the most important element in turning things around was the company's top leadership. "Good leadership at the top was critical in saving us. There was a clear message: We had to change or we'd be

---

*Lee Miskowski continued to have a very successful career at Ford. He retired in March 1994 after having served from May 1991 as the General Manager of the Lincoln-Mercury Division.

In June 1994, I was in Detroit and delivered a lecture to a large group, including many people from Ford and Chrysler. After years of red ink, both companies have recently enjoyed several years of high profits. People from both companies told me Entitlement had returned. Those conversations were impressionistic and didn't let me know in what ways or to what extent that's true. That input does, though, reinforce the idea that Entitlement is very difficult to expunge.

out of business. Then there was the meeting with the executives and Mr. Ford made his speech." Lee Miskowski picks up the story:

> Every four or five years we have a three-day meeting of our top 500 managers from around the world. . . . [At the meeting] in November 1984, . . . everybody really waited to hear from Henry Ford II. And when he got up to speak, he didn't talk about product, or economics, or profits, or any of the other things he could have chosen. Instead, Mr. Ford devoted his entire speech to one thing: our corporate culture. How are we going to live our corporate lives, and what values do we want to live by?

That speech galvanized the company. It inspired the articulation of the values statement that is now known as MVGP— Mission, Values, and Guiding Principles (see sidebar). It is not an empty document. It is, as Miskowski says, "our bill of rights and responsibilities," and it is the foundation of an amazing success story.

New Values in Operation

Miskowski relates some of the highlights of how they went about putting the guiding principles into action.

Quality

> That word is so pervasive in everything we do at Ford that we practically eat it for breakfast. And we mean quality in the broadest sense: every job, hourly and salaried, related to some aspect of quality. . . . It's amazing: When the quality is right (or at least improving) everything else seems to fall into place.

Customer Focus

> We're now running the business on the simple premise that we're here to satisfy our customers. And that

Figure 9-1. Ford statement of mission, values, and guiding
            principles

FORD

Mission

Ford Motor Company is a worldwide leader in automotive and auto-
related products and services as well as in newer industries such as
aerospace, communications, and financial services. Our mission is
to improve continually our products and services to meet our customers' needs, allowing us to prosper as a business and to provide
a reasonable return for our stockholders, the owners of our business.

Values

How we accomplish our mission is as important as the mission itself. Fundamental to success for the Company are these basic values:

People—Our people are the source of our strength. They provide
our corporate intelligence and determine our reputation and vitality.
Involvement and teamwork are our core human values.

Products—Our products are the end result of our efforts, and they
should be the best in serving customers worldwide. As our products
are viewed, so are we viewed.

Profits—Profits are the ultimate measure of how efficiently we provide customers with the best products for their needs. Profits are
required to survive and grow.

Guiding Principles

Quality comes first—To achieve customer satisfaction, the quality
of our products and services must be our number one priority.

Customers are the focus of everything we do—Our work must be
done with our customers in mind, providing better products and
services than our competition.

Continuous improvement is essential to our success—We must
strive for excellence in everything we do: in our products, in their
safety and value—and in our services, our human relations, our
competitiveness, and our profitability.

Employee involvement is our way of life—We are a team. We must treat each other with trust and respect.

Dealers and suppliers are our partners—The Company must maintain mutually beneficial relationships with dealers, suppliers, and our other business associates.

Integrity is never compromised—The conduct of our Company worldwide must be pursued in a manner that is socially responsible and commands respect for its integrity and for its positive contributions to society. Our doors are open to men and women alike without discrimination and without regard to ethnic origin or personal beliefs.

. . . is the single most significant event culturally that has occurred in our history. We finally have gone from a mentality that said, "We are smarter than the customer," to one that essentially is willing to admit that, in fact, we are not. And we now understand that it is the customer's interests—as complex as those interests may be—that we must listen and react to.

Of course, quality and customer focus are related, and Ford has recognized this link with its top-quality committee, a group that is charged with examining fundamentals. The group is divided into three subgroups, each one focused on one part of the quality strategy. The first subgroup defines quality from the customer's point of view, and feeds that to the second group, which is developing an internal system that allows the company to meet those customer expectations. The third group facilitates the changes in the corporate culture that are necessary for success in the quality focus.

Employee Involvement

We have learned some interesting things in the last few years. Employees have great ideas. Our new products have incorporated hundreds of ideas from the assembly worker on up. And of course this breeds pride and a sense of belonging.

It also breeds success. Ford has a plant in Batavia, Ohio, that manufactures a particular component also produced by a Mazda plant in Japan and sold to Ford. Ford leaders were thinking about closing down the Batavia plant because the Mazda parts were better and cheaper. Then, six months after the team concept started in 1985, the workers at Batavia saved their own jobs: Through employee involvement teams, they figured out how to make the part more cheaply than Mazda and of better quality.

As part of the employee involvement principle, Ford instituted Team Taurus; it is a fine example of a cross-skill team. Miskowski describes how it works:

Teamwork

The former way of cycling the development of a product from organization to organization (design concepts, advanced engineering, product development, etc.) and then finally hand it over to the assembly system and say "You build it" and to sales operations and say "You sell it" was thrown out in favor of a teamwork process. Now elements of every major component are involved in the entire process right from the beginning. The advantages are so obvious that one wonders what took us so long to come to this conclusion.

According to Miskowski, support for the team concept originated with then CEO Donald Petersen. In his speech, he incorporated this story from *AdWeek* magazine:

Petersen believes so strongly in the Team Ford concept that when *Motor Trend* magazine wanted to name him Man of the Year, he flatly refused the honor. Instead he put together a symbolic team with a member representing each department, from design to the production line, to accept the award. And, when the same magazine picked Taurus car of the year, award certificates were printed up for everyone who worked on the assembly line.

New Leadership

There appears to be universal agreement that the new leadership at Ford, embodied in CEO Don Petersen and President (now CEO) Harold ("Red") Poling, is truly different. Petersen recalls the old days at Ford, infamous for political infighting, personality clashes, bloody battles for power: "Those days built into me a strong desire to see things work differently."

And things indeed changed. Jack Telnack, chief of design, tells about the time Petersen looked over his shoulder at some preliminary designs and asked Telnack if he himself would drive a car like that. Telnack decided to be candid: "Absolutely not. I wouldn't want that car parked in my driveway." So Petersen told him to get busy and design something he would be proud of, and the result was the highly successful Taurus.

The Ford Philosophy Today

The question now is, Will this new culture sustain us now that we are experiencing hard times again? Overall, the mood at Ford seems to be "These are very tough days. But we've shown we can be winners. Let's weather it. Let's be very competitive."

The industry is cyclical and competition for customers, especially with the Japanese manufacturing presence in the United States, is unending. Despite the fact that Ford has achieved great gains in productivity, quality, and technology, in fact, Ford posted a loss of $884.4 million in the first quarter of 1991 and is not expected to show a profit for the year. We cannot know with certainty what its future will be like. It is not the only automaker in trouble. The Big Three U.S. auto manufacturers may have a combined loss of $3 billion in the first quarter of 1991. Sales are also down significantly for Toyota, Nissan, Honda, Subaru, Isuzu, and Mazda.

The transformation of Ford from Entitlement to Earning was a necessity in terms of achieving success in today's competitive marketplace. It enabled the company to triumph over competitors, especially with the Taurus, the most successful American car of the 1980s.

But transforming an organization's culture and structure does not insulate a company or an industry from hard realities that it does not control: The U.S. economy is in recession. Unemployment is rising and could reach 7 percent by the end of the year.

The banking system is in grave trouble, and so are major corporations. Eastern Air Lines and Federated Department Stores, for example, are in Chapter 11 bankruptcy proceedings.

The economic news is gloomy. Thus, consumers are not spending. They are not buying cars or much else.* Consumer spending is in one of the sharpest slowdowns on record and is a primary cause of the recession. The downturn has impacted virtually all regions of the country as well as most industries.

In this climate, about 20 percent of the banks have become "somewhat less willing" to make consumer loans. Car dealers report they are selling cars, but the deals fall through because they can't get financing. And consumers, who are laden with debt, are increasingly reluctant to borrow and buy as the Recession continues.

In 1990, over one million individuals filed for bankruptcy, and 1.2 million bankruptcies are predicted for 1991. Real incomes are declining. Cutbacks are continuing. Even people whose incomes place them in the top 20 percent no longer feel safe.

Those people are worrying about keeping their middle management jobs and about paying their mortgages and the costs of college. The 1980s psychology of affluence appears to have been replaced, at least for now, by caution.

Even though there's been a significant amount of economic recovery, the widespread loss of job security and the continuing downsizing by profitable companies has resulted in both con-

---

*What a difference a few years make! Arguing that the recession of 1990–92 created a large pent-up demand for new vehicles, Chrysler's chief economist Donald Hilty believes the industry hasn't reached the halfway mark in the recent business cycle. He expects sales of 16 million vehicles in 1994, 17 million in 1995 and 17.5 million in 1996. Though not quite as optimistic, the chief economists of Ford and General Motors also expect vehicle sales to increase.

sumer caution and spending. Helped by the recovery and low interest rates, people bought big-ticket items like cars and houses. As interest rates have risen, new home sales flattened and, in July 1994, even fell.

Thus, consumers are retrenching. No matter how vital your organization or how excellent your customer service or how exciting your product, as long as customers are worried and cautious, sales will fall.

But organizations, including Ford, which were in Earning, are far better positioned than those that never got there to recreate success when the economy, and thus consumer attitudes, improves.

Having survived the years of catastrophic crisis, Ford has learned some things:

- Because of the crisis, it was able to focus on quality and to get an excellent product.
- Relationships between people changed. You could see it at meetings.
- The winners, the people who keep getting promoted now, are the ones who espouse and support the new culture.
- Ford evolved a methodology based on consensus.
- There are teams of cross-functional people working together.
- The new hero transcends the narrow experience of the traditional kind of organization employees.
- People leave their old turf in which they've become mired and they move into new territory.
- Ford hires 5's, people who are driven not only by external rewards but also by internal passion.

One Ford executive comments on the depth of the changes: "The idea that employees should be empowered, that we need teamwork, and that management should be participative and involved was very new for us. There's still some tendency to go back to the old ways, but we're a much more democratic organization than we used to be."

We should also note the very positive changes in relationships between management and union. In the early 1980s, the United Auto Workers (UAW) was a very responsible participant in the renaissance. Its prime representative, Don Ephlin, was a "symbol of what can be." Today, people at Ford say relationships with the union were "never better." Management and the UAW work together in a sustaining relationship that is like nothing seen before. It's been a very positive development and is critical for sustaining excellence and success.

Part of the cultural change is using the minds as well as the hands of hourly workers. Management listens to suggestions from the blue-collar ranks and takes them seriously. At Ford these days, often you forget who's wearing the suit. Sometimes no one is.

Ford and the Earning Model

It's interesting to see how Ford insiders see their company in relationship to the Earning model. One Ford executive concluded:

> Before the crisis, Entitlement was very strong. Every employee expected a wage increase every year and they weren't shy about insisting on it.
>
> I think we started at 2. Then we had a three-year crisis and went to 9. We began the journey to recovery with Mr. Ford's speech. That helped get us to 8. Then we made the big changes we needed to and got to 5. We had successful products, we made a lot of money, and the media stories about us said we were the very model of what an American company could be if only they really tried. Of course, we had the advantage of almost going out of business!
>
> Unfortunately, we got to believing the stories and we slid to 4. We got a little too complacent. Then things got tough again and we went to 6. Now, after the last quarter's loss, we're at 7 or 8. We're not at 9 because we've been through this drill before! Right now, 7 is probably a very good place for us to be.

America's Future

As we know, in the years following World War II, governments, schools, universities, and large corporations gave employees essentially absolute job security. The experience of individual employees was so protected from the marketplace, from how well or badly their institution was doing, that the psychological awareness of Earning was lost.

We paid for that, painfully. Our organizations ended up with bloated and inflexible costs and with too many entitled people who, even if they were busy, were not productive. Then the economic barometer shifted, and the stranglehold of competition forced us to make changes.

In the new paradigm, the only way people should be able to get more is to produce more. The only way the nation or an organization can afford increased wages and remain competitive in an international market is for productivity to rise. While productivity has risen an annual 4.1 percent since 1979 in manufacturing, in the service and other nonmanufacturing sectors, where 80 percent of all workers are now employed, productivity grew at less than 0.2 percent a year over the same time period. Unless productivity increases significantly, our standard of living won't rise much. It could even fall. Therefore, in every sector of the economy, but especially in the nonmanufacturing sectors, productivity must rise significantly and swiftly.

We are on the right track. We are witnessing enormous changes in U.S. corporations. Management is shrinking because companies can no longer afford hordes of middle managers who crunch numbers and write reports. Management is also simplifying. Because it is clear that the fat belly of middle management slowed decision making, organizations are reducing the levels of management. It is a very fundamental change. It is a movement away from a hierarchical organization and a vertical distribution of power to a more horizontal organization.

In order to make that work, accountability will have to be direct and specified. But that is easily achievable because horizontal organizations tend to work and solve problems using small, autonomous business units. These small units are held responsible and directly accountable for real results. It's easier for accountability to be assigned, for goals to be defined, and for progress to be measured in small groups.

In the long run, if this change is deliberately managed, it will turn out to be very good news indeed. More people will have the opportunity to be leaders because every team needs a leader. Rather than a progression of promotions, most people will have a series of moments in the sun. Periodically, they will do special assignments, and lead project teams and ad hoc committees. Within successful groups, there will be both a hierarchy of responsibility—someone still has to be the boss—and genuine team interactions between people who are essentially peers.

In a more horizontal structure, where people are peers, everyone is presumed capable of participating and all are compelled to participate by peer pressure. Instead of just looking *up* to see what the boss wants, everyone is also looking *around* that round table. When people are peers, everyone has the right to pressure others to carry their weight.

In summary, then, the goals are to reduce the layers of management and institutional bureaucracy, to shift toward a more horizontal distribution of power, and to create teams of peers that have direct accountability. The results will be greater personal control and confidence; more initiative, experimentation, and risk taking; and great productivity.

Pushing power down and making people responsible and accountable will result in organizations that can compete, innovate, and flourish. That is the human base for a bright economic future.

America, go to work!

10

On the Personal Side

The psychologies of Entitlement, Fear, and Earning are not restricted to the marketplace. This chapter explores those attitudes as they affect our personal lives, especially within our families. The nonbusiness issue that comes up most frequently is parents' fear that because they did something terrible in rearing their children, the kids now feel entitled. Less common, but not unusual, people describe their elderly parents as being in Entitlement. It is much rarer that people express concern that a spouse, much less themselves, might be there too.

Many Americans are very upwardly mobile, far more successful than their parents were. But despite the success and the affluence, the great majority of them remain psychologically middle class. Psychologically middle-class people derive their sense of self-esteem and the largest component of their identity from their accomplishments. For them, the development of their capacities for excellence, the honing of their character, has been the result of the struggle to accomplish. Their pride is grounded in achievement.

Most psychologically middle-class parents, at whatever economic level, assume that will also be the route for identity and self-esteem for their children. The great majority, in fact, fear that without individual accomplishment their children will be deprived of esteem, confidence, and identity. They know the worst thing they could do is give their children too much protection.

Among the affluent, psychologically middle class, no family issue provokes more concern than how to provide for children without destroying them. In 1986, billionaire Warren Buffett announced that he wasn't going to leave his three children any money when he died. Why? Because he loved them. Rich people, he explained, and the children of the rich glibly point out the debilitating effects of welfare and food stamps on the people who receive them. But not many rich people make the connection to the reality that they are born with a lifetime supply of welfare and food stamps. The only difference is that their case worker is called a trust officer and their stamps come in the form of stocks and bonds.

One family I know created a family board that is parallel to the board of the family business. Requests for money from the children (who are in their thirties) are reviewed by the family board. Those requests are evaluated with the same kind of hard eye that the business board has.

In another family where the father is an entrepreneur with many businesses, the kids have been told "You will not inherit any business from me, nor will I give you one. I will, however, sell you one. The price will be fair and I will help you, but success or failure will be yours. You will have to deal with the consequences of what you do."

In still another family, there are three children. Each has an enormous trust fund but doesn't know it. When they graduated from college each was told "Get a job and learn what it's all about. When you've had some years under your belt come back and we'll talk about your working for me. But, understand, you're not inheriting these businesses."

Living in Entitlement

Entitled Children

We would all agree that our children are entitled to our love and a basic sense of security or well-being. Certainly I am not suggesting withholding those things from children. Entitlement, as we're using the term in this book, is not the result of parental generosity. It is, instead, the result of not holding people responsible for performance. It develops when there's no punishment when the achievement is well below ability.

Given all we know about the negative effects of Entitlement, why do we ever allow it to develop in our children? The answers are found deep in the human psyche.

Guilt is one very common reason. In the Introduction to this book, I recount the story of the stressed executive whose daughter haughtily informed him that he "owed" her a car because she had turned sixteen. Although he could not afford it, he bought it. Why? Because he felt guilty. He was afraid he'd hurt her in some terrible way because he'd divorced her mother and no longer lived with them. Because the car was too expensive and was a real sacrifice on his part, giving her the car was an important way to show her how very much he loved her. The car was an attempt to undo the injury he was afraid he'd created by leaving her.

When mothers stayed home, mostly it was fathers who felt guilty for ignoring the kids. Today, even if they are not divorced, both parents are usually employed, working hard and for long hours, so the potential for parental guilt is much higher. Parents may seek to gain the affection of their children and demonstrate their love by giving them things, often at a sacrificial cost to themselves.

Sometimes, out of misguided love, parents are too indulgent. They don't require good grades in school or a disciplined pursuit of athletics or a hobby. They say "I don't want my kids to have a hard time like I did. I don't want them to have to work as hard as I did. I want them to have a good time." That's why Entitlement particularly affects the baby-boomers, a generation who grew up in the decades of economic expansion after World War II.

Sometimes we don't judge, criticize, encourage, praise, teach, model, or require performance because we're not interested enough in what the other person is doing. The ironic result is that their demands often increase. In part, they're saying, "Pay attention to me."

We also create a psychology of Entitlement when we feel pity. When our expectations of people's ability to perform are very low, then we don't require performance. To require performance would be cruel. Very few people are comfortable being cruel, so instead we try to be kind. Sometimes we are too kind.

Entitled Spouses

While entitlement in families most often takes the form of indulging the kids, sometimes it's a spouse who is indulged.

Pat and Gary had been married for almost twenty-eight years when she moved out. While Pat had been unhappy for a long time, her leaving was still an awful blow to Gary, who felt rejected and abandoned. Nonetheless, while they were arranging the divorce settlement, he felt he had to be as generous in the divorce as he had been during the marriage. His self-esteem required that he continue to be indulgent to her. A corporate executive, affluent rather than rich, he had always financed a luxurious life-style that permitted her to remain at home.

They sold their house and divided all their other investments equally. He gave her first choice of all the things that two people accumulate in a lifetime together: the silver, the paintings, the furniture. Against the advice of his friends and his lawyer, despite the large amount of capital she now had, he volunteered to give her $7,000 per month in alimony.

Pat went from one end of the country to the other telling her friends how cheap Gary had been. "For all those years, all those rotten years, I should have gotten more." Treated for years as an indulged consumer, she feels so entitled to his earnings that she is not able to acknowledge his generosity.

Sometimes we don't require that people hold up their end, we don't act mad when they don't act responsibly, and we don't hold them accountable in the same ways as we do others, because we're afraid they'll reject us. That's especially true in the case of our emotional partners. Creating Entitlement in a sexual and emotional partner is understandable, but it is a poor life strategy. There's no gratitude for that sacrifice.

Entitled Adult Children

An old friend recently complained to me about her son. Mark was thirty-two and had never held a full-time job. He lived at home without paying rent. My friend had become very angry at him for not taking more responsibility for himself, but was torn by the fear that if she cut him off, they would both discover something they were trying to deny: Maybe he couldn't take care of himself. So my friend felt very ambivalent: She resented his dependence and was scared to death of requiring him to become independent.

Mark, too, has mixed feelings about their relationship. He feels that she owes him security because she is his mom, but he also resents the control she has over him because she acts like his mother.

He's very glib about why he has the right to live in his mom's home. He has a thousand excuses, most of which blame others, or accidents about why he doesn't have a serious job. Under the slick excuses, there's tension. He may not consciously realize it, but he's afraid that if she pushed him out he wouldn't be able to manage.

Then there is Cecilia, who managed to remain an undergraduate for nine years. She enrolled in all of the math and statistics classes that the University of Massachusetts offered. Semester after semester, year after year, she'd enroll in five courses, drop two, get a B in one, a D in another, and flunk the third. The next semester she'd re-enroll in the course she had failed and the one in which she got a D. She managed to take some courses three or four times.

Her family supported her through all those years. In fact, they never asked anything from her, even though her education took more than one-third of the family's income. Cecilia wasn't required to do anything. She didn't have to contribute any money and she wasn't required to produce grades as a condition of staying in college.

The parents' generosity stemmed from pity. They couldn't put it into words, but they felt she was fragile and vulnerable. They assumed she would fail, in every kind of way, if they stopped supporting her. Therefore, they collaborated with her evasion of the tougher judgments of the marketplace by financing an endless education.

Because Cecilia never held a job for all the years she remained in school, her relationship with her parents remained that of a child. She never experienced herself as their peer, capable of earning a living and creating an independent life for herself, and her parents never learned to respect her.

People who have earned their way, especially under difficult conditions, may love others even when they don't perform, and they may feel compassion for them, but they will not respect them. People with a psychology of Earning require that others have that same attitude as a minimum for respect.

Thus, parents of adult but dependent children are very likely to feel terrible conflict, especially if the parents are in Earning. On the one hand, they know their continued indulgence of dependence and entitlement is bad for their child. On the other hand, and appropriately, they're terribly scared of the consequences of withdrawing their support or requiring performance as a precondition for support.

Mark and Cecilia's parents were convinced their children couldn't deal successfully with adult reality, a reality which assumes you can and will take care of yourself. Once we assume incompetence, we expect failure. And then we get failure. There's a powerful relationship between the level of performance expected and the level of achievement delivered. When we presume incompetence, unwittingly we create incompetence.

Unrealistic Goals

People who are in Entitlement don't know that's where they are. Because they believe they're owed what they get, they don't bother with thanks. Especially if the giver is in Earning, they are extremely exasperating.

Adults in Entitlement are also frequently annoying to others. For example, they tend to have either no ambition or have unrealistically high goals. They can be very frustrating to deal with as they exaggerate their competencies and ignore their actual deficiencies. They talk excitedly about high ambitions and rationalize away the reasons they've never succeeded. Not only are they typically unaware of their attitudes of Entitlement but they often appear to deny their repetitive failures or nonperformance.

Arnold, at age forty-three, has been overly protected all his life. From nursery school on, his adoring mother has passionately explained away the reason for his failures. "His kindergarten teacher was a frustrated old maid who took it out on the kids. His college professors were all foreigners and none of them could speak English. His boss was a flake with a terrible wife."

On the other hand, she also always assumed that he would fail. Therefore, she and everyone else who was close to him were certain that he'd always need support, psychological and financial. That's why they never challenge him, never dispute his explanations of failure, and generally tolerate his boastful assertions.

He set out to become an architect but he never quite made it. He got the degree after an extra year in school, but he wasn't able to do the years of apprenticeship training required for a license because he couldn't stand working for someone else. Paradoxically (but understandably, because he has no confidence), he insists on being the authority, the boss. Unable to practice as an architect, he decided to become a developer. He told everyone that all the other developers had cookie cutters for brains; he would create something unique.

In the ten years since he graduated from college he's never raised any money for any venture and he's never held a job for more than a year. He has never earned even an average income, but that doesn't stop him from thinking up new projects. He appears not to have a clue as to why no one invests in him. He uses psychological defenses to both blind him to his failures and to create the feeling that he's a big shot.

He putters his way through life. He always looks busy, but he never grapples with what's real. There are no deadlines. He continually postpones decisions. His goals are big but vague and there are no timetables. In that way, he avoids assessing a life that has drifted into middle age.

Now that he's over forty, even his mother acknowledges something is wrong. All the people who care about him feel frustrated. They'd like to shake him by the shoulders and yell "Look at yourself! Grab hold. Get a job. Go to work. Grow up!" But they don't say anything. They sense his vulnerability. They continue their support with only occasional outbursts of impatience or anger when their patience has worn thin.

For Arnold, the psychology of Entitlement has now become a defense against the psychology of Fear. As long as his psychological defenses allow him to perceive himself as entitled, and as long as he can avoid realistic assessments, he postpones his awareness than he is scared to death.

When People Are Victims

We are more likely to sustain Entitlement in people when we believe the reasons for it originate from conditions outside of their control. When we see the cause as visited upon someone, then we see that person as a victim. We don't hold victims responsible for their nonperformance, and thus they are exonerated by those who would otherwise require performance. In addition, once the victims accept the idea they're victims, they have a reason for why they should be excused from normal requirements of responsibility.

The earlier in life the idea of victimization begins, and the longer it continues, the greater the chance that a critical phase in development is passed and movement from Entitlement to Earning becomes impossible.

The way we manage our lives, the means by which we survive, the hurdles we overcome, the accomplishments we achieve, the quality of the work we do, and the ways we deal with what is real are how we earn self-esteem.

Changing Old Patterns

Getting to Fear is never the end goal, but sometimes it is a necessary step in the journey to competence and independence. Without the external pressure of the end of support, Mark and Cecilia are extremely unlikely to leave dependence and Entitlement.

In each case, a judgment call must be made. Could the person who is not performing adequately become adequate under different circumstances?

If the answer is "no," the decision may be made to continue

the support. If the answer is "yes," the conditions that foster dependence and entitlement have to be changed: Mark has to leave his mother's house and survive on his own by getting a real job or be hungry. Cecilia needs to learn that her parents will pay for two more semesters of school and none after that.

When we change the conditions that create Entitlement, we know two things will happen: (1) The person with a psychology of Entitlement will not believe conditions are really changed. Those with the power to alter the conditions will have to make the changes very clear more than once. Leaving Entitlement is not accomplished in one stroke. It's not an act, it's a process that won't be straight or smooth. (2) The person (or people) who imposes the changes will be afraid and ambivalent. That's why a clear understanding of why the conditions of Entitlement are being changed is essential. The person must also be prepared for the recipient's increased fear and attempts at greater dependence. The recipient is very likely to also feel resentment and anger.

Living in Fear

Unlike Entitlement, most of the people who are in Fear know it. The levels of emotion they're experiencing are too great to be controlled. If anything, they feel as if the emotions are controlling them. The amount of emotion is palpable. That's why responses in Fear tend to be more extreme, exaggerated, inexplicable, even bizarre, compared with those in Entitlement.

The lack of confidence in Entitlement results in attempts to avoid situations in which a realistic assessment would lower even further the person's low sense of self-esteem. The lack of confidence in Fear leads to efforts to diminish the amount of emotion being experienced and to create a sense of being in control.

Short-Term Fear

Unlike Entitlement, people can be in Fear because of a short-term change in external conditions. We've all had experience with situations that have created acute stress. Then, the realistic and appropriate response is Fear. In an unfortunately common situation today, for example, many people have become fearful about their jobs as their organization:

- Downsizes because of a shrinking market share;
- Flattens its hierarchy to become more participatory;
- Merges with a competitor and ends up with redundant employees;
- Moves manufacturing offshore; or
- Sells divisions.

Where there had previously been Entitlement or Earning, external conditions have created an internal state of Fear. In fact, Fear is the psychological healthy response to these conditions.

While feeling Fear under these conditions is an appropriate response, people differ a lot in terms of how they handle it. More than a matter of style, this tends to be an issue of confidence. Those who have had a psychology of Earning have an advantage because they're confident.

Tom, age fifty, is married to Lydia, an upper-level manager for General Electric. Three years ago he was fired from his job with a huge auto-parts distribution company because he was within six months of being eligible for the pension plan. Tom and Lydia recovered from their shock in short order and filed a lawsuit against the firm. In the face of his dismissal they got energized instead of debilitated. They also won a large settlement.

It took a while, but he got a job with his former employer's biggest competitor. Helping the new company win was an exquisite pleasure. He was a success very quickly and within a year he was slated to become a vice-president. For two years he looked and sounded great. "How are things?" I'd ask him.

"Hard," he'd say. "The whole industry is being squeezed by competition. But we're getting better all the time. I'm really making headway in getting the changes made that we need."

Then, to his shock, his whole department—sixty-seven people—was eliminated.

Today Lydia is beside herself. "Do you know what he does?" she said to me. "He reads all day. He stays home and he reads. He talks about going into business for himself but he doesn't do anything. I keep asking him if he has a business plan for this week. He always says he's going to make one up, but he doesn't. He just sits in his chair. I say to him, 'What would you do if I made $25,000 a year instead of $80,000?' He just says, 'But you make $80,000.' "

She's furious because he looks, to her, as if he doesn't care about getting a job. Because he doesn't have obvious symptoms—he's not crying or having trouble eating—she doesn't see he's suffering from huge amounts of fear and depression. For the moment, he's coping as best as he can.

Before he can put himself back into the marketplace he has to be in a state of less emotion. Age fifty, fired twice in three years, a man whose confidence has been battered, an expert in an industry that's going downhill, he is scared and sad. He can't do much until he's in less emotional turmoil. Until then he's unable to leave his chair and battle the world.

Another common external condition that takes people into Fear is divorce. It's especially likely for women because fewer women than men remarry. And fewer women than men earn enough to create the life-style they had before the divorce.

Ruth married a man who had inherited enough money that he never needed to work. Their major income came from his investments. She worked part-time as a librarian. They always had full-time household help, a magnificent house, and their own tennis court. They also had Entitled children. The children grew up in a universe in which adults catered to the pleasures of children and children were never required to do anything in return.

After many years, the couple divorced. First Ruth experienced loneliness. Then she learned he'd been spending his capital for years; there wasn't much left. Even working full-time, there was no way she could afford the life she once had. The divorce took her into Fear and the kids further into Entitlement.

Her world is a maelstrom of high emotion. She feels fear for herself, anger at her husband, and guilt about the kids.

"What," she asked me, "can I do? The kids manipulate me and I know it. I'm exhausted."

"Sometimes," I said, "it's peace at any price. Seems to me, that's where you are. When you're feeling better you can start picking up the pieces and straighten the kids out. Give yourself time." In a few years, she'll probably be fine.

Long-Term Fear

With time, people who normally coped can be expected to recover from the extreme of emotion. That's not the case when people's psychology of Fear is the result of a chronic state of high anxiety. When there have been high levels of Fear for a long time, reducing it is much more difficult.

Ben, for example, was a reasonably successful print salesman for thirty years. Married, he had three children and had always been actively involved with them. When the children married and moved out of town, he always chatted with them on the phone at least once a week. By the time he retired at fifty-eight, he had five grandchildren whom he adored. He enjoyed traveling and made a point of taking two vacations a year, at least one of which was overseas. He enjoyed his friends and saw them two or three times a week. He liked to cook for friends, he liked to fish, and he loved to read.

By the time he reached seventy, he had become a very different man. He stopped phoning his children and his grandchildren. He no longer traveled. He stopped entertaining. He stopped seeing friends and justified that by criticizing them. "You can see them," he'd tell his wife, "but don't bring them here. I can't stand them."

The process of deterioration took years. The erosion of his personality was so gradual that the changes were subtle. Friends would say "Have you noticed that Ben doesn't seem to want to go out the way he used to? Have you noticed or is it just me?" Most people said, "Oh, he's all right. It's just his way. It's the way he is."

Gradually, the geographic area he was willing to venture out in got smaller and smaller. It was defined by an area he could walk to. After a while, he would only leave his home if his wife was with him. It was only by cajoling him that she got him out at all.

What was going on? Very slowly, Ben, who had lived a normal life, had become phobic and obsessive. Trying to reduce his acute but vague sense of anxiety, he created a tiny and rigid universe. As long as his wife stayed in that universe, his controls controlled her life.

Since the deterioration was so gradual, neither of them realized that his behavior was abnormal. That's why they never sought help in changing it. While she tried for years to get him to do things she knew he'd always loved, she couldn't succeed. She tried logic and reminiscence. They don't work against Fear.

When high levels of Fear have become chronic, they're not amenable to reduction through reason, affection, obligation, or familiarity. Mental health professionals are needed to provide both support and challenge. Without that kind of intervention, there is a good chance the pathological behaviors, which are the evidence of psychological defenses, will get more and more irrational.

Living in Earning

I've hardly ever seen a parent whose kid was in Earning who didn't take credit for it. For myself, I think it's mostly the kids's doing and not the parents. Parents can't push or haul a kid into Earning. What they can do is communicate their high expectations about what they think their child is capable of, express their pleasure when the expectations are met and their disappointment when they're not, create circumstances in which children experience the results of what they do, and foster conditions in which they are responsible for performing.

In my own experience it's not a matter of telling them what to do as much as it is an assumption of competence. Appropriate to their age and abilities, children are held responsible for themselves. Parents facilitate but they don't do for the kids and they don't excuse nonperformance. They *love* unconditionally, but they *like* proportionate to behavior.

Billy, a third-grader, came to visit me recently. I hadn't

seen him for a year. As I expected, he'd grown a lot, but I hadn't expected a big personality change. He'd always been shy and distant. Now he was bubbly, talkative, and forthcoming. I asked his parents what had happened.

> He goes to private school, and for the first two years, the school is basically lenient and forgiving. The principal says the kids mature at different rates and much of the bad behavior disappears as the kids grow out of it. He always acted out a lot, he was the class clown, and his grades were terrible.
>
> We were all waiting for him to get his act together, but it wasn't happening. Then just before Christmas last year, when the first semester was almost over, the principal and his teacher called us in for a conference. They said he had until the end of the next term to get his grades up, or they were "sure there were other schools that would be better for him."
>
> Now we took it seriously. We told Billy he had one term to get it together or he would have to leave the school he loved. Then we asked him what he wanted to do. He said he wanted to stay. We asked if he'd work really hard and he said yes. We told him we'd help him. None of us knew what we were in for.
>
> It's one of the hardest things we ever did as a family. First, we had to find out if there were any reasons why he didn't do better. It turned out he has some learning disabilities. They're the kind you grow out of but that doesn't help him now.
>
> We hired a tutor for him, a woman trained in special education. She came over, after school, three times a week, four times a week during the summer. She drilled him over and over until he had it. She gave him techniques for learning and made him practice over and over. And while [his dad] is on the road most of the time, I sit with him after dinner, every night, and we go over his homework. Sometimes we're at it until 10.

Most of the stuff the tutor had him do would help in the long run, but it didn't do much for the immediate present. His father decided they needed a goal for right now and he made it spelling. Billy had a spelling test every week. His father told him, "You are going to get 100 percent on your spelling test every week, starting next week."

"I don't think I can do it," Billy said.

"Oh, yes you can," his parents replied. The three of them focused on spelling. That became the first subject he did in his homework. He studied the words and then his mother tested him every night. When his father called from out of town, he asked how the spelling was going.

The first week, he got the 100 percent. And the week following that he got 100 percent. Spelling was becoming an area of triumph. He looked forward to spelling. Beginning with spelling, he was learning to concentrate and work hard. For the first time, he was earning academic success. Of course, it was terrific.

Every term, in every grade, there was a special spelling test. The words on it were hard for adults. Billy's father told him he was expected to get 100 percent on it, just like all the other spelling tests.

"I can't," Billy said. "No way. Nobody gets all those right."

"*You* will," his father replied, "because you can." He was the only kid in the whole grade who aced that exam. His confidence soared.

Billy's father said to me:

> You know the message we tend to give our kids because we want them to be confident is "You can do it. It's easy. You won't have any trouble with it. And if you don't do it, we'll love you anyhow." The Japanese give their kids a different message. They say "You can do it, but it's going to be hard. You're going to have to work very hard. And don't even think about not doing it. That's not an option."

It isn't easy to require performance just as it isn't easy to require that your children stand on their own; psychologically it is often much easier to protect them, take care of them, do for them, excuse them, and even ignore them. Requiring responsible behavior means you have to be involved in defining what is expected, you have to decide what the parental role should be, you have to evaluate what they do, and you have to deal with your disappointment and their resentment when the evaluation isn't totally positive.

Perhaps most difficult of all, when you insist that your children be responsible for what they do, is that you can't remain the nonjudgmental nurturant and loving parent of infants. After earliest childhood, to a large extent, the parents' role changes into that of a teacher, a guide, a coach; on the one hand, enthusiastic and encouraging, and on the other, demanding and unsentimental.

Many years ago, when I was a divorced single parent, my son dropped out of college. He had decided to pursue a career as an auto mechanic. It was not in my power to make him stay in school. I couldn't say, "Stay in school or else!" because there was no "or else." If he left school he'd earn his own living. If he left school I'd still love him. Besides, if your goal is to make people responsible for themselves, in principle as well as in practice, you can offer an opinion but you cannot tell people what to do. You can however, help them to realize the consequences of a choice they're making.

With difficulty because I adored him, with discipline because I adored him, I said:

> You're going to do what you've already decided. I know you've not been happy in school. On the other hand, I don't think being an auto mechanic is such a great choice. I want you to know what it's really like being an auto mechanic. You cannot move into this house. You have to have your own place that you pay for and you cannot eat more than one meal a week here. You're going to live on what you earn. Give me a hug! Good luck. Now I guess you'd better start by finding a place to live.

It takes hundreds, perhaps thousands of such experiences in the years of growing up, most of them vastly less dramatic than this one, to create a psychology of Earning. The earlier it's achieved, of course, the easier it is to maintain because there's a core of confidence and an expectation of success.

The people with a psychology of Earning have an advantage: They are more likely to succeed, even when initially they fail, because they are adaptive. They are the people who are more likely to learn from error and failure because they perceive what is real and they change course when that's called for.

Where people with a psychology of Entitlement are clustered, the demands for Entitlement increase. Where many people are in the psychology of Fear, it is a short step to panic. When the clustering is of Earning, the synergy leads to the highest levels of energy and purpose.

Having a psychology of Earning and being in circumstances where Earning is considered the ideal enable people to live their life in an endless process of learning and developing. From a psychological point of view, there's nothing better.

11

Questions and Answers

In the past years, I have presented lectures, seminars, and workshops on the concepts of Entitlement and Earning to many of our largest corporations. The format is often rather informal, and questions are common. Although the companies are very different, the questions are remarkably similar. Here are some of the most frequently asked.

Q: Why is it that to move from Entitlement to Earning you have to go into Fear? Isn't that counterproductive?

A: No. It's essential.

When people have been in Entitlement, especially very deep Entitlement, any movement toward a higher level of risk—even if only a tiny bit higher—feels like Fear to them. Out of Entitlement, the only direction you can go is toward Fear. One way to visualize this is to think of the original bell-shaped curve as a three-dimensional figure (see Fig. 11-1).

You need a level of Fear to provide the motivation to change. General Motors, the world's largest corporate bureaucracy, is beginning to change its traditional adversarial relations with at least some of its workers and to emphasize cooperation instead. Where once workers were required to shut up and follow orders, now they're being asked to think. A team of hourly and salaried employees managed to cut the number of parts in the rear doors of Cadillacs and Oldsmobiles from fifty-two to thirty. That reduced the number of stamping dies from ninety-three to thirty-eight, and the

Figure 11-1. The Earning curve model in three dimensions.

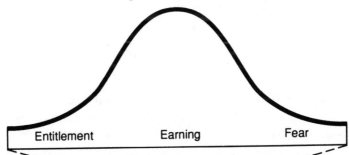

Think of the model in three dimensions.
Bring the ends toward each other.

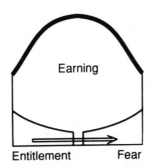

Because any risk is scary, those with a psychology
of Entitlement invariably go into Fear when performance
requirements and accountability are imposed.

number of presses from ninety-three to ten. The company
is saving $52 million a year.

What made the workers want to change? Did they have
a deep inner desire to be empowered? Hardly. The change
is the result of fear. All 310,000 plant workers knew that
40,000 GM workers had been laid off.

People resist change; they also tend to regress, slipping
back to a way of behaving from the past in which they felt
more comfortable. That's why Entitlement continues to
flourish. Thus, when leaders require performance whereas
they didn't before, they are pushing people into Fear.
When they do that, morale plummets: "The leaders of this

place haven't a clue as to what to do. You should have been here in the old days."

This makes it very tough on the leaders. It's hard to sustain the discipline of requiring performance in the light of the bleak mood, especially after the Country Club of Entitlement. But that *must* happen, because the whole drive will be to slide back to Entitlement. Many organizations that were in Entitlement in the 1980s tried to impose requirements of achievement. They instituted all kinds of new systems of evaluation and compensation, but they failed to move into Earning because the leaders lacked the courage to stand fast in the wake of falling morale. The organizations fled back to Entitlement.

The result is that Entitlement is more secure than ever, because when leaders institute new requirements of performance in the future, no one will believe them. It is necessary that requirements for performance be sustained and acted upon so that people learn that the good old days are really gone.

While I was explaining this model in a recent workshop, I noticed one vice-president vigorously nodding his head. "Yes, yes!" he said, "that's what I use!" I asked him what he meant. "I keep pushing and pushing my people, driving them harder and harder, until I know I'm driving them too hard and then I pull back and relieve the tension."

"How do you know where that point is?" I asked.

"I feel it. You just feel it. It's in the air." He paused and then added, "But when you're right in the center, boy, what a high! You're right on your edge, you're pushing as hard as you can. That's when it's exciting. And good."

Q: Will employees resent the corporations as we begin to move them out of Entitlement?

A: Yes.

Q: But don't you run the risk of destroying people's loyalty when you push them out of Entitlement? Surely that's not good for the company.

A: There is no question that finding the balance point can be rather tricky. You don't want to deliberately push people all the way to extreme Fear, to 9, because they become paralyzed. Of course, sometimes external events push them there, but as a deliberate strategy it's foolhardy.

I think that management has to be careful and cautious before they overturn value systems like "The HP Way" or IBM's "Respect for the Individual." These are enormous cultural values that have been critical in creating employee commitment. Pressure for performance, but don't jettison these policies.*

Q: Can you have a system that works without horizontal peer pressure?

A: I don't think so.

Q: Why isn't Entitlement a problem in Japan? The Japanese have job security for life—and nothing is more entitled than that—and yet they have the highest productivity in the world.

A: Simple. Japanese firms are famous for pressuring for performance. They have unbelievable peer pressure and also pressure from their hierarchical management.

Interestingly, Susumu Tonegewa, Nobel laureate, has suggested that the qualities that have made Japan an industrial power may be the very ones that make "Japan's science . . . definitely inferior to America's in terms of real creativity." Those qualities include deeply ingrained traditions, acquiescence to authority, strict seniority, little debate, and an immobile work force. They often generate loyalty and teamwork but they don't create far-out, far-ranging break-

---

*While it is true that those values did contribute to employee commitment, I underestimated the extent to which IBM's "Respect for the Individual" and "The HP Way" also contribute to a sense of Entitlement. Observing both companies, I find that's especially true in those parts of the organization that feel most besieged. IBM's Lou Gerstner has jettisoned the corporation's old values, including "Respect for the Individual," and substituted eight new operating principles. Instead of "Respect," Gerstner says "We are sensitive to the needs of all employees and to the communities in which we operate."

throughs. As Tokyo University researcher Zenichiro Honda said, "We don't understand in our hearts the joy of taking risks every step of the way."

Q: Where does responsibility lie—with the individual who expects Entitlement, or with the company that allows it?

A: Both.

Q: How long would it take to change a corporation?

A: At least three to five years—unless there's a crisis.

Q: I'm a 5, maybe even a 6, and I'm working in a department where everyone, including the boss, is a 2. How can I get them into Earning?

A: Chances are, you can't. You're not the boss so you don't have the power you need to galvanize energy, require performance, and so on. You'll certainly need a powerful ally to do that.

Of course, you can try. You might begin by talking with the boss and others who are powerful. Your arguments would include the ideas that the department is less productive than it could and should be, and that there's more fun for everyone when people experience the achievement that results from successful risk taking.

But you are already a model of the kind of performance, energy, and risk taking you're advocating and the department has not changed. It has not become more like you.

Without a crisis in which it has become obvious that their ways of operating are ineffective and unproductive, the probability of your changing the culture of the department is small. And, without backing from the boss, it's impossible.

A better strategy would be to leave the department and find an organization where there's a better fit between its culture and your personality.

Q: Why is teamwork counter to a top-down organization?

A: Because in a top-down organization you defer to levels, to someone at a higher level than you, and teams are made of peers.

Q: When people in a work unit have an attitude of Earning, but the boss is still a bureaucrat, how can we protect them? Eventually they'll end up challenging the boss on bureaucratic nonsense. Then what?

A: Some managers still have the mentality that "I know best and you better not question it." When someone does question them, they tend to mutter "I'll get that guy." Until the whole culture begins to change, that person's best strategy is probably to leave. The best thing would be if he or she is really terrific at the job, so that the loss creates a real problem for the manager. Sometimes that's what it takes to shake up people.

Q: I'm the manager in a company that went from a 1 to a 9 practically overnight as a result of a merger. It's taken my department a year and a half to get to 7. We still have a couple of supervisors who are back in the old days of Entitlement. Can I fire them, or should I eliminate their jobs?

A: While they are surely irritating to have around, I'd be very careful about firing them. What you would mostly accomplish is to push people further back into Fear. After very high levels of fear, increasing people's sense of fear is not a good idea. The recovery from 9 to 7 is recent and probably fragile. It is more important to further reduce everyone's sense of risk than it is to be rid of two annoying supervisors.

From a strategy perspective, an important question is how other employees perceive the supervisors in question. If others view them as hard workers, if they're held in general affection or respect, if the prevailing attitude toward them is positive, I'd try to change their behavior without resorting to the extreme of pushing them out.

If they are not regarded positively, there are more options, including firing them. That's especially the case if the general view is that they're not pulling their weight under the new and tougher conditions and that management is basically fair. But even then, there's a judgment call about whether firing them would increase the general anxiety level, which would be counterproductive.

I would not recommend eliminating positions as a way to fire people when the department is still recovering from the cynicism, rumor-mongering, and mistrust of high anxiety. Eliminating positions as a mechanism to fire people is an obvious technique and will only increase the mistrust from which the department is recovering. People will say "You can work here for ten years and just like that they get rid of you!"

Q: Why do people think they're in Earning when they really are in Entitlement?

A: Because they're busy.

Q: Making the assessment seems tricky. I'm thinking of some specific individuals. I think I've got them figured out and then one day they look very different.

A: Sometimes people can look as though they alternate where they are on the curve, most frequently between points 2 and 8. But, the points are consistent psychological states or attitudes and you don't have real swift alternations, only apparent ones. Most often people have moved from 2 to 8, and they're trying to cope with the anxiety by insisting they're entitled. It is as though they're trying to deny the change, but the denial is a response to the elevated anxiety level.

Sometimes a person looks like a 2 with peers or the manager and like an 8 with a higher-level boss. That person is probably really a 2, and just very, very careful to stay in the good graces of the superior.

Of course, an extreme set of circumstances, such as being asked to make a presentation to the CEO, could easily take someone into Fear who is normally in Earning. But, in general, people are more consistent in their responses than they are variable.

Q: In terms of where they are on the scale, are people the same in their personal life as they are at work?

A: Generally speaking, yes. I think there's consistency proportionate to the level of confidence. People who have earned confidence in one sector of life are better able (though it's not an absolute given) to intersect in other aspects of life from a base of self-esteem. Similarly, those who have been unable to develop confidence in any major sector of life will, most often, try to avoid situations in which there is real competition and assessment. So people who are fearful at work are not likely to be courageous in other spheres. Those who are confident at work are likely to face all their world with some degree of confidence.

Q: Does the size of the organization determine where that organization is on the curve?

A: To a degree. It's true that you're far more likely to get Entitlement in larger and richer organizations that don't need full-out effort from everyone—or didn't used to. Similarly, it's easier for Entitlement to develop in the bureaucracies of large institutions, whether corporate, government, health, or education. And you're more likely to have Fear when there isn't much of a financial cushion and when there isn't a legacy of lifetime employment. More frequently that will characterize smaller organizations, ranging from mom-and-pop operations to entrepreneurial high-tech start-ups.

And, of course, organizations tend to attract people whose attitude or relationship to risk is compatible with that of the organization. We would expect, for instance, that the old AT&T would have attracted large numbers of people for whom security was the dominant motive; by the same token, the start-ups in Silicon Valley are home to many who thrive on risk and excitement. In that sense, the size of the organization has some impact on where on the curve people will tend to be.

The concepts and the Entitlement to Earning model can be applied to organizations of any size.

Q: Is it possible that different segments of the company are at different places on the curve?

A: Yes.

Q: I'm not sure that I can apply your model to my own situation. I work in a very small department; there are just four of us and we're all pretty autonomous. I'm not really responsible for anyone else's contribution.

A: The value of a model is that it helps us understand and make sense out of what we are seeing, so even though you may not be responsible for others, in the sense of being their manager, you can have a fuller understanding of why they work the way they do. You can use that understanding to help create a more effective department, perhaps in informal, even subtle, ways.

For more than twenty years, I was on the faculty of the University of Michigan, and for three years I was also an associate dean there. In my personal office, there were four of us: an assistant dean, an executive secretary, a clerk, and me. While, in a sense, everyone worked for me, in fact we had different jobs and no one really worked for someone else. We were, like your department, basically autonomous.

We were all at least reasonably productive, but our styles were very different and we were at different points on the curve.

The assistant dean was serious, hard-working, competent, thorough, and dependable. He had mastered all the rules and requirements. Whenever there was a sticky question about whether or not a student could graduate, he was the court of last opinion. He most loved using the details he had already learned. He was uncomfortable with abstractions and liked change in small amounts. He didn't like to make big decisions. He was a 4.

The executive secretary was staggeringly competent. She was awesome. She said, "My job is to protect you so you can do the things that are important," and that's what she did. She answered my routine correspondence using my words, my style. She typed, she edited, she critiqued, and she suggested. She took care of clients and made sure nothing important ever fell through the cracks. She never had to be told what to do; she was there before I was. She was a 5.

The clerk was a kind, sweet woman for whom there were never any emergencies. She had one pace, slow and steady, and it never varied. She never made mistakes, partly because she never tried anything new. To get her to learn to use computer graphics, we finally had to tell her that if she didn't get sharp on the computer we'd have to let her go. We knew she could do it. She just had to be showed into the twentieth century. She was a 3.

And then there was me. In the three years I was in that office, I never did learn the rules of graduation and never intended to learn them. My job, as I saw it, was to be the catalyst for change. Of course, that's how I saw the job because that's my personality. I don't like repetition and detail. I love change and the big picture. I'm a 6.

The model helps me to understand our styles, the sources of our pleasures and frustrations. I don't think either the clerk or the assistant dean would ever be likely to pursue risk by themselves. But where they are on the curve suggests that if some risk taking were required of them and support were provided, the outcome might well be positive. And I think it's really useful to know that the 5 was the secretary and not the boss!

Don't forget that you can also use the model to improve your own performance. For me, it's useful to be aware of a tendency to not have a lot of respect for progress in small increments. I have to pay more attention to those opportunities; in that sense, I have something valuable to learn from the assistant dean.

Q: I can see that how you structure the compensation system would have a powerful influence when you're trying to make changes. Could you summarize how this works at various points on the spectrum?

A: First, when an organization is in Entitlement, it's necessary to use an evaluation and compensation system of significantly different rewards and punishments, of clear winners and losers. In fact, under these systems, winners benefit at the expense of losers and the system creates losers.

Ranking or a forced distribution are ways to achieve this winner/loser structure. Ranking always produces the lowest 5 to 10 percent, and a forced distribution (a bell curve) sets out the percentages of people who are allowed to be outstanding (it's never more than 10 percent) and the percentage who are required to be unsatisfactory (typically 5 to 10 percent). We use systems like these to prod employees out of their complacency.

When the organization (or substantial numbers of its employees) is in Fear, that system of required losers as well as winners, of significantly different punishments and rewards, must be maintained, despite the fall in morale, because it's part of the forced journey from Entitlement to Earning. If the pressure were reduced by eliminating the differentials, the response would be a return to Entitlement.

However, there is one exception. If the level of Fear has remained high long enough so it has become a chronic state instead of a crisis peak, if Fear is no longer being experienced as part of a journey but has become a debilitating and oppressive constant, then it's necessary to decrease the level of anxiety. You don't want major differentials in compensation and you don't want a system that requires some people to be losers. At that point, across-the-board salary increases or merit-pay adjustments are appropriate. Evaluations should not require fine distinctions. Instead, assume most people will work somewhere within a broad band of acceptable performance and use just a few categories of performance.

In an experimental program, Cyanamid no longer uses a recommended distribution. Instead, the great majority of people are designated G, for good, a very few people are E, for exceptional, and another very small group are U, for unacceptable. People in the program are pleased to report they find this system less arbitrary than the previous conventional one.

Now, when the organization is in Earning, you don't want a system that requires there to be losers. Here the goal should always be to have as many winners as possible. Therefore, in Earning, the requirements of performance can be set very high, but there is no arbitrarily set limit on how many people can reach or exceed the targets or goals. IBM's 100 percent club is a model of that. To get into the club, you have to hit 100 percent of your target, but there are no limits on how many people can get in; it works so well that many exceed 100 percent.

In Earning you can end up with people evaluated in a range from unacceptable to outstanding, and that means you can get a range of rewards and punishments, but that's the result of people's performance and not the result of an imposed procedure such as ranking or a required forced distribution of performance appraisals.

In Earning, as in Fear, there should be just a few categories of performance, maybe three. Many possible categories will set people against each other in a purposeless competition. When organizations select and train outstanding people, when they retain only outstanding people, and when those people have a psychology of Earning, the distribution of performance will not and should not resemble a bell curve. It will be skewed to the right, toward excellence.

To summarize, differential rewards have to be used where there is Entitlement. Forced differentials, in the sense that only some can gain them ("If I win, you lose"), should not be used where there's Fear because that increases anxiety. They should not be used in Earning because that is where you want to have many earning success.

Q: Is it possible that the model could be applied to other kinds of problems, aside from the business world? I am especially thinking about the public school system, because of my children, but it seems it could be applied to other general issues as well.

A: Remember what a model does: It simply provides a framework, a perspective, for thinking about issues and, ideally, seeing them in a slightly different way. In that sense, the

Earning Curve model becomes a useful tool for analyzing several significant issues of our time.

The school system is a big one, to be sure, mostly because of the effect of tenure systems. I believe it also helps us think about Entitlement programs like union pension funds, about government welfare programs, and even about global economic systems. I think it's not unreasonable, for instance, to characterize certain communist countries as economies that are in Entitlement.

Of course, these issues are enormous and complex, and to really look at them takes far more time than we have here. If the Earning concept contributes toward change within U.S. organizations, the purpose of this book will be fulfilled.

Part Two

Finding Comfort in Endless Danger

12

The Borderless Economy

In the last few months I've had three conversations that I never imagined I'd have. The first was with a man whom I'd met about a year ago when he was the executive vice-president for human resources of one of the Fortune 100 companies. Although he had personally engineered massive downsizings in his own company, he was bitter and bewildered as he told me he'd been laid off in a restructuring and forced out in an involuntary "voluntary" early retirement. He called me because he was networking, trying to use even our slight acquaintance to find a job. One year ago, he was a man at the top of his ladder, totally unprepared to be judged and jobless.

My second conversation was with an old friend, a man who had been a professor at the University of Michigan and is now a professor at the University of California in San Diego. He's internationally famous, a world-class researcher, and has been a tenured full professor for more than twenty years. He called to say the university was applying enormous pressure on its senior faculty to take early retirement and leave. It had become so uncomfortable, in fact, that he had decided to take the early retirement. In the academic world, no one ever imagined circumstances in which preeminent professors could be shoved out.

My third conversation was with my eldest daughter, a pathologist who works in a university hospital. Unfortunately, that involved a long commute and she decided that was making things hard for her family. When she told her chief she'd decided to return to private practice he asked her to stay, but said it would be okay if she left because he knew six pathologists in town who were looking for a job. Then she said, "You know, there's no more security working for the hospital than there is in private practice." No one would have thought that MDs could be looking for work.

Today, about half the people who are unemployed are white-collar professionals who never conceived that they could be out of a job. And the other 50 percent are unemployed blue- and pink-collar workers who are for the most part not returning to their old jobs even as recovery replaces recession, because their old jobs are gone forever.

What is happening? On one level we could say there's enormous pressure everywhere to get costs down and that's what's driving the changes. Indeed, that is true, and we can see the largest amount of change has taken place—and continues to occur—where profit and loss are both really important and easily visible. That's why corporations have changed vastly more than any other kind of institution, and it explains why our governments and school systems have talked a lot and changed so little.

But there is a reason for the relentless pressure on costs. That reason is critical to our understanding why unpredictability is replacing predictability and insecurity is replacing security. The core reason for these changes is that technology has created a *borderless economy*. I recently had a small experience— it was nothing much—but now I really understand what that means.

This little anecdote begins with the fact that my lawyer and I had been negotiating for months with a company called Qualtec. Qualtec does training and we were trying to come to an agreement which would allow them to teach my material presented in this book. When we first began discussions I envisioned a simple relationship sealed with a handshake. Instead, as the lawyers worked on the contract, the clauses and compromises got more elaborate because we were into heavy issues of ownership, territory, obligation, and the like.

We were pretty close to having an agreement when I happened to be visiting my son. He lives in Naples, on the west coast of Florida. Qualtec's headquarters are in North Palm Beach, on the east coast of Florida. My lawyer is in San Diego, because that's where I live. My publisher is located in Manhattan.

It was late in the afternoon but just approaching 2:00 P.M. in California. My son said he was starving and wanted to go out to dinner, which meant leaving his office. "Peter," I said, "you know I can't leave. This is the phone number I gave my lawyer and I don't want to miss this call." Peter smiled at me with excessive kindness and said, "Welcome to the twentieth century!" He put his phone on call-forwarding, clipped his beeper on his belt, slipped his small portable phone into his shirt pocket, and we left.

Picture it: We're walking slowly down the street in Naples, going to a restaurant, and suddenly Peter says, "A call is coming through." Still strolling the street, he pulls his phone out of his pocket, turns it on, listens for a minute, hands it to me, and says, "It's your lawyer." Ambling down the block, I listen as my lawyer describes the latest issues that had come up and we decide what we should do. Then he says, "I think we've about got it. Agree? Okay. Are you ready to be patched in?" I had no idea what that meant but I say, "Sure." What it meant was that within 30 seconds—no more—he had created a conference call. Now Qualtec and my publisher are also on the line.

Walking down the street in west Florida I was talking with Qualtec on the other side of the state, my lawyer in San Diego, and my publisher in New York City. We could as easily and as swiftly been talking to anyone, anywhere.

A borderless economy is one in which every nation and every organization has lost the protection of distance. It does not matter where you live; it does not matter where you work. Your colleagues can be anywhere. More important, your competition can be anywhere. And, as the protection of distance is gone, so too, is the protection of time. Communication, anywhere, is instantaneous. Technology has removed the safeguards of distance and time with the result that competition is increasing geometrically.

In a borderless economy, pressure on costs is unremitting because customers have easy access to your competition. Increasingly, customers will assume product excellence and personalized service because those, too, will be offered by the competition. A borderless economy makes it much harder for organizations to develop a strategy that makes them stand out.

There is no going back. This is not incremental change. The world has begun a vast quantum change. The past is not a prelude to this present. This present may not predict the future. Welcome to the new world!

Where conditions created Entitlement, Entitlement persists as an attitude and a set of practices. But in a borderless economy, no one can afford the costs of Entitlement. As organizations find themselves in endless competition, everyone will find they're under relentless pressure to demonstrate that they do add value, that they do *earn* their salary, that they are competitive when they are evaluated against others. Earning in the Age of Uncertainty is replacing the Era of Entitlement.

This is a watershed time. I mean that now and into the future, things will be more and more unlike what they were. There will be no more comfortable pauses in which we can lean back, smile, and say, "I got it." Endless competition and relentless change are hard to deal with, and are especially difficult for those who enjoyed the complacent, risk-averse, and safe conditions of Entitlement.

Getting to Earning

In the very competitive world of a borderless economy, it's necessary to be in the sector I call Earning. In 1992, the American Management Association conducted two surveys that tested the validity and usefulness of the model I put forth in this book. The first survey reported responses from 408 human resources managers, and the second analyzed feedback from over 1,000 secretaries. Remarkably, the surveys found a powerful correlation between how profitable an organization was and where it fell on the earning curve. Unprofitable firms and nonprofit organizations were in Entitlement. Highly profitable organizations were described as being in Earning. That is, very profitable companies were likely to have many of the characteristics of Earning and unprofitable organizations have many qualities we find in Entitlement.

In profitable companies, people were not bound by strict rules and regulations. People responded to that by being proactive and by being accountable for their productivity. Highly profitable companies tended to be confident, innovative, and risk taking, and they exuded energy. They encouraged people to work together, count on each other, and bend the rules or make new ones. In Earning, these companies required performance and were innovative, focused, and energetic enough to keep advancing. That's why they were very profitable.

Unprofitable companies and not-for-profit organizations, on the other hand, had many of the qualities of Entitlement. With little confidence in the organization's ability to solve problems and little confidence in subordinates, employees avoided risks, didn't innovate, and weren't flexible. Performance requirements and levels were low, as were morale and the motivation to perform. People were neither accountable or empowered. Those organizations tended to have low levels of energy, and despite their objective lack of success, people in them tended to feel complacent.

Alas, whether in Entitlement or Earning, whether profitable or unprofitable, a hefty percentage of organizations were described as bureaucratic.* Since *Danger* was first published, I've become aware that the most insidious, subtle, and expensive forms of Entitlement are hard to discern. They involve people being very busy—shuffling paper, getting signatures, writing reports, going to endless meetings—in activities that consume resources but don't matter. What's scary is if you ask these people, "Are you working?" they'll say, "Hell, yes! Like a dog!"

That idea is nicely summarized this way: imagine a person pushing hard against a large rock. The equation goes, **Force** times **Distance** equals **Work**. *Force* refers to how hard one pushes or how much time and effort you put in. In an Entitle-

*32.3 percent of the highly profitable companies and 54.3 percent of the unprofitable companies were described as bureaucratic in the second survey.

ment culture, people are praised and they assume they'll be rewarded for putting in time, for trying, for pushing. In a competitive world, the only thing that matters is *Distance,* how far the rock moved. *Work is moving the rock.* That's the only thing that counts. Therefore, challenge every action by asking, will this move the rock?* If the answer is "no," you probably shouldn't be doing it.

"Does it move the rock?" has become a widespread shorthand for asking if something really matters; it has become a test of whether or not to do something. Steve Mason, CEO of Mead Corporation, ordered a huge rock, about 650 pounds, to be placed in the lobby of Mead's headquarters building in Dayton. The vice-president of human resources of Rohm and Haas, Marisa Guehren, gave all of her subordinates a present of a small rock. "That way," she said, "you won't forget."

After *Danger* was published my colleagues and I created a questionnaire to measure where organizations are on the Earning curve. We assess thirty-four variables (shown in Figure 12-1). While organizations have a tendency to be in one part of the curve more than in the others, they are never entirely in a single sector.

The most common condition I find in organizations today is that along with high levels of anxiety, cynicism, and fear, the Entitlement culture remains very powerful. Thus the most common organizational task today is to manage when levels of *both* Entitlement and Fear are too high.

We find that even in Fear, organizations with a history of Entitlement remain in Entitlement to some extent. Typically that involves continuing to avoid risk, treating small innovations as though they were big breakthroughs, ineffective performance evaluations, maintaining the bureaucracy, compensating poor and outstanding performers roughly equally, a lot of trivial or worthless work being performed, and expensive processes like quality improvement becoming more complex and separated from business goals.

Even where there have been years of churn and turmoil

---

*Until the organization's culture has moved from Entitlement to Earning, I'd direct the question to the action rather than to a person because people in Entitlement naturally master the explicit and implicit rules of that code.

Figure 12-1. Thirty-four variables for measuring where a
company is on the earning curve.

Risk management	Response to innovation
Customer information	Emotional climate
Organizational control	Performance evaluation
Response to mistakes	Attitude toward honest
Business ethics	expression
Attitude toward change	Team work
Initiative	Use of power
Leadership behavior	Leadership control
Energy	Excellence required
Employee evaluation	Bureaucracy
People development	Job security
Commitment to organization	Compensation
Promotion policy	Empowerment of employees
Worthwhile work	Recognition
Fair treatment of employees	Trust
Political style	Problem solving
Quality improvements	Honesty
Follow up	

and red ink and downsizing, Entitlement is amazingly difficult
to eradicate. In May 1994, Louis Gerstner, CEO of IBM, announced the results of an internal survey of 1,200 top managers. Forty percent of that group still didn't accept the need for
change in a Big Blue that has been struggling since 1986. It is
proving to be immensely difficult to change seven decades of
an entrenched, patriarchal, Entitlement culture. After being on
the job more than a year, Mr. Gerstner observed that "When it
comes to being a results-oriented corporate culture, we're not
there yet, not by a long shot." The Big Three auto makers illustrate the same point. Even with the example of GM before
them, even after their heroic measures to gain solvency after
terrible losses, both Ford and Chrysler have regressed to aspects
of Entitlement now that they're profitable.

As the world has become very competitive and security is
threatened or lost, people feel fear, dread, and anxiety that
causes them to cling as best they can to any of the safety of

Entitlement that they can find. Thus, the most common organizational task today is to manage when levels of *both* Entitlement and Fear are too high. Observing the sustained resistance to giving up Entitlement, I've come to conclude that while *individuals* might be successfully impacted by psychological pressures or human resources programs, *organizations* require more powerful factors than those to get them into Earning. The factors needed to change organizations are the subject of the next three chapters.

13

Get Real

Since the first edition of *Danger* was published, I've watched many organizations try to transform themselves. I now believe there are three primary things organizations must do. Those are (1) Get real; (2) Operate in optimum ways; (3) Create critical conditions. In this chapter I'll deal with the first.

Getting Real involves:

- *Urgency*
- *Leadership*
- *Strategy*
- *Pressure to Perform*
- *Purposeful Work*

Urgency

More than anything else, organizations have to get their people in touch with reality, because it's reality that is driving the need for mega-change. Entitlement protects people from reality; it provides comfort even when the organization is failing. I was at a division of IBM when the corporation was losing billions. When I asked the managers what their biggest problem was, they said, "We only have 3 percent raises to give out."

Organizations need a sense of *urgency* to remain in Earning or to justify the end of Entitlement. The urgency must be real. It needs to come from the recognition that today business is endlessly competitive, demanding, and difficult. *Urgency is the natural motivator for change,* and it needs to come from everyone being in touch with the reality of the market, with market conditions and outcomes, with competitors as well as with customers.

When he was IBM's senior vice president for human resources, Gerald Czarnecki told advanced management classes, "Leave here with the mindset of an entrepreneur running a five-person company who wakes at night with one great fear—the fear of not making payroll. That's not only his greatest fear, it's also his greatest strength. Every manager must be a little hungry and a little scared." The best organizations have the culture of an entrepreneurial start-up: successful enough not to be running too scared, but scared enough to focus on what matters and *do it!*

The only factor that justifies major change and disruption appears to be a sense of urgency. When organizations try to create change by executive fiat and human resources programs like ranking, performance evaluation, and compensation, the required changes and human resources programs are resented and resisted because, without urgency, they seem arbitrary and therefore unnecessary. No major change efforts should be started before the urgent reasons for change can be articulated convincingly. Executives must be able to explain the reasons why the situation is urgent and the ways that change will create positive outcomes if they are to get acceptance and support from management and other employees.

Leadership

Moving from Entitlement to Fear, from Fear to Earning, or staying in Earning in tumultuous times requires effective *leadership*. Leaders must create the vision, by which I mean the answer to the question "What business are we in?" In a swiftly changing, borderless economy, the answer to that question is continuously changing. Deciding on the business of the business is the first step in setting priorities. Leaders have to set clear priorities. Without clear priorities, efforts are splintered, and little is achieved. And leaders create strategy—what the organization will do to achieve a market advantage.

It's currently fashionable to talk about team leadership rather than the leadership of individuals. When the world is scary and the future is uncertain, people have an emotional need for a leader, a person whom they can trust and to whom they want to make a commitment. They want a person they can believe in.

It is then a critical responsibility of leaders to project a conviction that they know what to do and that success is achievable. Leaders have to make people believe that the hard journey of change and transformation is not only urgently necessary but will lead to something worthwhile. Leaders have to inspire confidence in people who are racked by doubt.

When anxiety, fear, uncertainty, and ambivalence prevail, leaders must *act*. When anxiety levels are high, not deciding and/or not acting increases people's sense of uncertainty and decreases people's confidence in the leader. Lou Gerstner said of IBM that the length of time spent in trying to create the changes it needs is as dysfunctional as the required changes are serious. Gerstner observed, "The answer to morale is action."

Alas, many people now in positions of leadership are the wrong people. There are great differences between peacetime and wartime leaders. Most of the people who climbed to the top of their ladder gained their years of experience in the era of Entitlement. Entitlement conditions breed managers whose style and preference is to avoid dangerous risks and hard choices. In this post-Entitlement period when conditions are intrinsically unstable and risky, organizations need wartime leaders. Those are people who are really comfortable with risk and change, because they perceive turbulent conditions as filled with opportunity.

Leaders lead because they convince others that they understand the issues better than anyone else. People follow them because they speak about solutions with persuasive conviction, because they act decisively, and because they project confidence when others are uncertain. The prototypical leader is Winston Churchill who said when England was expecting the Germans to invade, "We shall fight on the beaches, . . . we shall fight in the fields and in the streets, . . . We shall never surrender."

Ultimately, leaders lead because they create a passionate

commitment in other people to pursue the leader's strategy and succeed. In the end, leadership is not intellectual or cognitive. Leadership is emotional.

Strategy

An especially significant responsibility for an organization's leadership is the creation of *strategy*. The organization's strategy is the means by which it will achieve success. Strategy defines the primary competitive advantage on which the organization will focus. Strategy identifies what the organization will emphasize in terms of what it offers to its customers.

Strategy is not long-range planning. The latter consists of specific, detailed, and pragmatic schemes to reach goals. In contrast, strategy is conceptual; it's the big picture of how the organization will differentiate itself from other organizations by offering something especially desirable or valuable to its customers.

The first question that has to be answered is "What business are we in?" The second question is "What is our competitive strategy?" The answer to those two questions sets the direction and the priorities of the organization. In today's borderless economy in the midst of turbulence, the strategy must be convincingly shrewd, aggressive, advantageous, and achievable.

Strategy must be conceptualized from the point of view of the customer. According to consultant Michael Treacy, there are only three possible foci in terms of gaining a strategic advantage. Those orientations are to have:

1. The lowest cost
2. The best product
3. The best service

A choice must be made between these orientations because they are intrinsically contradictory. For example, an organization can't have the lowest price while providing expensive service and breakthrough products. While organizations must be outstanding in one focus they must also be adequate competitively in the other two. Therefore, an organization that chooses a strategy of the best product or the best service must usually also control their costs. Treacy adds that achieving a leadership position in any one approach takes such a high level of concentration and energy that it is very difficult for an organization to focus on more than one approach at the same time.

There's often a basic confusion between the strategic position or focus and how it is achieved. For instance, Total Quality may well help to improve a product and achieve a lower cost. But the customer doesn't care *how* the outcome was achieved— only that it was and therefore something of greater value is offered.

The process of achieving the strategy must not be confused with or pursued as the strategy. The processes include improving how the work is done; improving the market and delivery system; improving financial effectiveness; and improving the synergy of the parts. Here are specific examples of the processes:

1. Improving how the work is done: TQM, empowering employees, creating teams, reengineering, centralizing or decentralizing, partnering.
2. Improving the marketing and delivery system: JIT, information technology, new retail channels, advertising, changing the structure and/or mission of the sales force.
3. Improving financial effectiveness: downsizing, capital investments, vertical integration, outsourcing, creating alliances, getting suppliers to cut prices, making R&D focus on commercial products.
4. Improving the synergy of the parts: realigning people and their mission, reorganizing structures, changing compensation from individuals to teams or units, improving communication, changing management's style.

It is critical that everyone be aware that the goal of these processes is to achieve the strategy. That is, strategy delivers *operational excellence, product leadership,* or *customer intimacy.* That's what the customer buys.

Pressure to Perform

Earning organizations are results oriented and people are under continuous *pressure* to achieve their goals. Pressure involves
making every person and every unit accountable for performance. At the individual level it involves goals, performance evaluations and feedback, coaching, compensation, and the criteria
for promotion and other forms of recognition. At the level of
business units, pressure is exerted by monitoring revenue, cash
flow, market share, and customer satisfaction. When IBM reorganized and created Workforce Solutions, a business that sells
human resource expertise within and outside of IBM, the unit
was told that either it would be profitable or it would be gone.
This was a radical change from the past when all unit's financial
results were pooled.

Increasingly, organizations are trying to link people's compensation and other rewards to important outcomes. That
means there will be no more meaningless "attaboys," no more
banquets for seniority, no more years of chair-hugging, and no
more cross-the-board bonuses to everyone. That is, people will
not be rewarded when they haven't performed. It also increasingly means that everyone has some amount of pay actually at
risk.

An effective compensation practice involves tying part of
an employee's compensation to individual performance as well
as to how the corporation did. Some corporations, including
Eastman Kodak and Primerica, are requiring their directors,
executives, and managers to own significant amount of the
stock so people really are managing their own money. Safeway's
CEO required his top five executives to give up bonuses they
had already earned when profits fell by 20 percent. He told
them, "When shareholders lose, managers should lose." I was
at a meeting with Conrail executives when they decided employees should have part of their pay at risk. While the idea was
revolutionary, the amount was only 3–5 percent and that's
probably too small to affect behavior. IBM now has half a billion dollars or 4–5 percent of their payroll set aside for variable
pay. Each business unit is supposed to designate the two or
three performance goals which if they were met would earn

employees a payout. IBM is shooting for 10 percent of people's compensation to be linked directly to performance. That is seen as a critical tool in undoing people's sense of Entitlement. I agree but think the percentage needs to be greater.

Pressure must be greatest where the outcome matters the most. The definition of what is really important must come from a clear understanding of what's most important to the business. Anything that isn't central to the business of the business or the strategy of the business is automatically less important.

Most people don't understand that. Employees view all parts of their jobs as equally important and management evaluates all aspects of people's performance as though all of the parts were alike in value. That's never true. People have to know what really counts.

My favorite example of the critical importance of what matters most, comes from academia. When I was a brand new faculty member in the psychology department at the University of Michigan, my chairman told me that I would be evaluated on the basis of three different activities. The three kinds of work were service, teaching, and research. When he gave me this information, he was also implicitly giving me advice. The way he said it, he was telling me to be good at all three. He made it sound as though they were weighted equally. That wasn't true. Big time.

Years went by and I had become a full professor and an associate dean of the college. Now I was one of the people involved in making decisions about who got tenure. Tenure is one of the most important decisions made in a university because it pretty well determines whose going to be in an academic department—and who won't be—for about the next twenty-five years. Because departments tend not to grow much, the number of positions doesn't increase. The decision to grant someone tenure is also a decision to exclude anyone else.

On what basis did we grant tenure? On the basis of outstanding service to the department, college, university, or of the profession? Hardly. On the basis of teaching? We denied tenure to some people who had won teaching awards. What really counted? What business is the University of Michigan in? It is in the business of creating information and knowledge. There-fore, of the three activities, research is far and away the most critical part of one's job.

But that still doesn't answer the question of what would earn someone tenure. Would it be the number of publications or the quality of the journals or the number of invitations to speak or the value of research grants? Those count. But they're not critical. Keep in mind that tenure grants a job for life. Ten-ure is a strategic decision because the university's competitive edge is in producing breakthrough information and tenure will ultimately determine the direction and the quality of the re-search of a department for a generation. On what, then, does tenure depend? What really matters?

While the quality and quantity of research and publications counted, the critical variable was: Does this person's work lead you to believe that they are likely to be in the forefront of their field for the whole of their career? If research is your business you can only afford to keep the people who will continue to do breakthrough work for the whole of their career.

Purposeful Work

Earning cultures are results oriented so that all activities move the rock. That means everything that people do is *purposeful;* their actions make a difference. They don't put energy or time into "garbage." Garbage is all the stuff people do that uses up resources but doesn't make a difference.

A simple test of whether or not something is garbage is to ask if a customer would be willing to pay for it. If a customer wouldn't be willing to pay for that activity, there's a good chance it's garbage and shouldn't be done.

Until IBM discontinued the practice in the winter of 1994, in the midst hemorrhaging red ink, they continued to have phone-mail checkers. The job of the phone-mail police was to call IBM numbers and be sure the messages were perfect IBM-speak. That is not only a blatant waste of resources, it is also not a job for a grown-up person. Even if the message was not IBM-perfect, who cared? The work of the phone-mail checkers wasn't *work*. It was garbage.

Jene Stead, the president of AT&T's Global Communications Systems Unit, which makes office phones and equipment, makes sure that meetings move the rock. He says, "I say if you're in a meeting—any meeting—for 15 minutes, and we're not talking about customers or competitors, raise your hand and ask why. If it goes on for half an hour, leave! Leave the meeting!"

No matter what they do and no matter where they stand on the status ladder, everyone wants their work to matter, because if it doesn't, a big part of their life is insignificant. People want their work to be purposeful. They want it to matter enough that there's an intrinsic reason why it should be done with quality. When your work is important and it contributes to something important, you are very motivated to do that work as well as you can.

Reengineering is a complex and difficult process of analyzing how work is done in order to eliminate garbage. When it is effective it results in extraordinary increases in efficiency. But reengineering is expensive and successful in only 20 percent of the reengineering efforts. Therefore, I'd recommend an initial approach to eliminating garbage that's simpler.

Very simply, ask people what are they required to do that is unnecessary. Give them permission not to do those activities, or encourage them to simplify their work processes for a week or two after which the effects will be assessed. Encourage people who work together to discuss the value of what they do and how things could be simplified or eliminated.

Ask people to keep a detailed journal for several weeks of exactly how they spend their time and what was the outcome. For example, I might note that every Monday I went to a two-hour staff meeting but, on average, only 37 minutes were devoted to important business issues. I might learn that a third of my department's time was spent in producing splendid reports that had little impact. I might also learn that less than 15 percent of the sales calls I made on the phone generated new business, but when I showed up in person that percentage went up to about 27 percent.

Everyone then needs to answer the questions, "If you had 5, 10, 20, 30, 40, or 50 percent *less* time, what would you stop doing?" And the reverse, "If you had 5, 10, 20, 30, 40, or 50 percent *more* time, what would you do more of?" Everyone must focus on doing only that which moves the rock. Organizations can afford to do only those activities that contribute to the success of strategy in the competitive milieu of a borderless economy.

I'd like to note that a possible outcome of eliminating garbage is eliminating jobs. It would take an extremely optimistic person to expect people to cooperate in eliminating their positions. Most of the time, therefore, a necessary ground rule is that getting rid of busywork will not result in people losing their jobs.

14

Operate in Optimum Ways

Operating in optimum ways involves:

- *Values*
- *Simplicity*
- *Selection*
- *Effective processes*

Values

Tom Whiteside left IBM to join Silicon Graphics. He said, "Nobody's dumb at IBM. But it's like herding cats; they all have their own agenda." Being individualistic and competitive can foster creativity and innovation. But it can also stifle cooperation and coordination. Effective organizations need to have room for individuality, and they must also, simultaneously, reinforce the *value* that contributing to the common good must often take precedence over seeking advantage for a part. The values of the organization must motivate people to work for the good of the whole.

Michael Cavanaugh, an adjunct professor at the University of Massachusetts, organized his twenty-nine MBA students into four teams who were to use Lego blocks to build scale models of buildings on the campus. The students became totally absorbed in the task and worked on the models evenings and on weekends. Despite a heat wave of more than 100 degrees in buildings that weren't air conditioned, the students "donated

our lives to this," observed Norman Duquette, a participant.
Constructing the models was hard because the students had to
use the architectural blueprints for the real buildings. Therefore, Cavanaugh asked everyone to share their knowledge of
engineering. He said, "But there wasn't any sharing. Once they
learned how to build a wall or a corner, that became a corporate
secret. I wouldn't be surprised if some of these guys want to
take out patents on their projects."

When Ray Smith, CEO of Bell Atlantic, asked his top 130
people when they had felt most committed, they all identified
times when they had had the opportunity to tackle jobs that fell
entirely within their functional responsibility. Smith finds that
that response poses a real problem. Meeting companywide
goals is still less important to his executives than meeting their
own objectives. Today, he says, you must have people who will
sacrifice their individual gain for the goals of the team.

This is also an issue for unions. Obviously unions developed because workers needed to confront management's
power. Today I would argue that in the long term neither
unions nor management can afford to continue their traditional adversarial stance because their collaboration is critical to
beating the competition. The future actions of the unions need
to come closer to collaboration with management because, ultimately, corporate job security depends on business profitability. Profitability requires a flexible and adaptive labor force that
is committed to moving the rock.

At the signing of the Declaration of Independence, Benja-
min Franklin said, "We must all hang together or, assuredly, we
shall all hang separately."

Organizations must be without internal boundaries. No
one can afford the competition and duplication that inevitably
results from internal silos and the territorial attitude that "it
wasn't invented here." As external competition continually increases, most competitive energies must be directed outward, to
beating the competition. While some internal competition is
useful because it fuels people's motivation to be outstanding,
for the most part internal relationships must be collaborative.
The wagons must form a circle. The group must be able to
become a team.

A group is not a team, even if the group is small. A group continues to operate on the basis of traditional hierarchical power, in which power is distributed vertically and the top of the pyramid tells the rest what to do. In contrast, a team is organized on the basis of horizontal power. When power is distributed horizontally, it's distributed on the basis of knowledge and skill. Horizontal power is a critical element of both the empowerment and team work. The need for a commitment to the good of the whole is greater where there is a horizontal distribution of power. That's because power, derived from knowledge and skill rather than a formal position actually creates a more competitive situation for with horizontal power the distribution of power is flexible rather than fixed.

Of late, management has focused on the benefits of teamwork in contrast to the gains from individualism. We must beware of faddism. The focus on teams is a natural response to their absence when the focus is on individuals. But don't throw the baby of individualism out with the bath water. Teamwork has moved to center stage for at least three reasons. One, with tremendous pressure on costs in a borderless economy, there can be a significant cost advantage with a workforce organized in self-directed teams. Teams can be flexible, cost effective, and efficient because any individual's skills and knowledge is available to all members of the team. An empowered team, operating with horizontal power, uses its human resources more productively than happens with vertical power.

The second reason for the focus on teamwork is that collaborative team members can produce more effective and innovative solutions to problems than when people work individually. The College of Literature, Science, and the Arts of the University of Michigan was run, with horizontal power, by six deans and six members of the executive committee. It always impressed me that whatever position anyone held at the beginning of a discussion was always different from the one they took at the end.

The third reason for focusing on teamwork might be the most important. As the organization's strategy must focus on *creating* an outstanding outcome for the customer, so the values of the organization must focus on *delivering* that outcome to the customer. When the focus is on solving a customer's problems, the work unit has to become flexible, cross-functional, and include people at different levels of the hierarchy, which are the characteristics of teams and teamwork.

Let's imagine that you are a physician in private practice and you have just moved from Chicago to San Francisco. One of your first tasks is to set up a telephone system in your home and in your office. You call Pacific Bell and ask to speak to a rep. You're looking for someone who knows everything there is to know about telephone equipment and what you're most likely to need. You want to get all the information you need to make choices, and you want to do that with one conversation. You want to make your selections, and then you want the company to make them happen.

You don't want to make a second call, much less a fifth. You don't want to know that the telephone installers are mad at management and aren't showing up on schedule. You don't want to learn that headquarters and the people in the field are not communicating with each other. You don't want to discover that the software developers are behind and the features you thought you bought aren't ready and no one knows when they will be. You don't want to have to learn the business of the phone company in order to solve the problems of your business.

In a borderless economy, if customers don't get what they want from one vendor, they'll "let their fingers do the walking" and they'll go to another. It's that simple. That's why organizations must present a seamless face to the customer as they solve the customer's problems.

Simplicity

Entitlement cultures create Entitlement solutions. That means their programs, processes, performance measurements, plans—everything—are as long, detailed, and complicated as possible. What was designed to be a solution to a problem becomes, instead, a deterrent to achieving something—or it becomes a source of new problems.

Anything complex lends itself to becoming an Entitlement activity in which more attention is given to process, or how things are done, than to product, or what is done.

AT&T, for example, had a performance evaluation form in which each variable was weighted proportionately to its importance. It took me four readings before I had any idea of what was being assessed. The resulting data were so complicated they were useless. The federal government's personnel rules take 10,000 pages, which makes it impossible for anyone to know what the rules are. Traveler's Insurance created a grid of twenty human resource variables. The desire to be inclusive destroyed any possibility of having a focus. IBM had a training module to teach empowerment. It was 60 single-spaced pages. Empowerment means, "See what's important and do it!" There's no way that simple idea could survive 60 pages.

Complexity creates murkiness. Therefore, plans, processes, goals, performance measurements, strategy, language, and communications—everything—must be as *simple*, clear, and brief as possible. Brevity and simplicity require precise clarity. Clarity is the best demonstration that anyone really knows what they're talking about.

I have a favorite comparison between clarity and opaqueness. On a recent trip to the British Museum in London my husband bought a full-size copy of the Magna Carta. The Magna Carta is one page, 20⅛ inches wide and 13⅛ inches high. In contrast I give you the Clinton health care proposal, which is 1,368 pages long.

Selection

No matter how long the runway, a pig can't fly.
—Kirk Lawrie,
President and CEO,
Richmond Savings

Training is frequently expected to do more than it can accomplish. Training can teach, and it is especially effective when the skills and information to be taught are concrete and specific. Training is less able to teach more complex and abstract skills. Training, for example, will probably be more successful with a higher percentage of people when teaching *reading* than when dealing with *communication*.

Training *cannot* do what many people are expecting it to do, which is to change adult personalities. Adult personalities don't change very easily or swiftly. The new demands on training reflect either a fundamental optimism or an unwillingness to accept the reality that it's hard to get adults to make core changes. The more extreme the personality, the more unlikely it is to change.

The current focus on getting training to change personality arose because there's been a fundamental change in the kinds of attitudes and behaviors organizations want from their people. It wasn't very long ago that we defined an effective manager, executive, or leader as a person who told others what to do. In other words, people in positions with power had to be comfortable directing others. If they didn't tell others what to do, but instead created more give-and-take interactive relationships with their subordinates, they were in danger of being dismissed as wimps. This was an especially dangerous style for women who tend to prefer collaborative rather than confrontational exchanges. Now, as we all know, the "feminine" preference for horizontal or shared power is being articulated as the preferred style in many organizations.

Now we're saying that effective leaders motivate people by empowering them. We want people in powerful positions to listen to others' input. That's very different from the directive management style most people learned and with the authority many managers believe they've earned. The male manager who told me, "The Golden Rule is he who has the gold, rules," is not going to be changed into a person who shares power by three days of training. When having and using power is an important part of someone's self-esteem and a central component of their identity, training cannot alter that.

For decades we hired people and told them to master the procedures and learn the rules and obey them. We protected people from change and encouraged them to avoid risk and to do what they were told. Now we're telling people we want them to be creative, innovative, and to challenge those above them. People who are highly experienced in avoiding risk are not going to be transformed from chickens to lions in a week of training. Even those who rappel down the cliff in Outward Bound are more likely than not to regress to their previous risk-averse style when they return to the office.

In most organizations we praise, reward, and promote individuals. Now we're saying the best people are team players. We're asking people to change from being competitive with each other to being collegial. Only confident people are able to share with others. Since training doesn't bestow confidence directly, it will not alter the personality that hoards information and other forms of power in endless competition with everyone else.

Because there are limits to what can be achieved with either experience or training, the company should first *select* people who already have the desired qualities, and then have those attributes honed in training and through experience. And as it is critical for organizations to do what they say, people who are in positions of leadership and decision making must be models of the qualities employees have been told are the most desirable. And it's not only necessary to *select* the right people, but to *de-select* those who used to perform acceptably but who now, as the criteria have changed, embody unacceptable behaviors and attitudes. *De-select* means replace.

Effective Processes

Organizations have many systems. We have systems, for example, to do the following:

- Increase quality.
- Hold people accountable.
- Measure performance.
- Compensate for achievement.
- Reengineer how work is done.
- Increase the span of control.

- Create teams.
- Empower people.
- Train people.
- Create upward feedback.
    And so on.

These systems are *processes*. Processes are the methods we use to achieve goals. Processes must never be confused with goals. The goals of an organization must always be business goals. For example, executives have told me their goal is to create an organization made up of empowered people who work in teams. While that might be a tremendous, high energy, collaborative place in which to work, that can't be the organization's goal. The goal must be a target in the business of the business.

In addition, the justification for a process must be in terms of a business outcome. Finding that empowered people make more decisions and enter more freely into discussions isn't an adequate argument to justify empowering people. The justification for empowering employees has to be that the discussions conducted by empowered employees lead to better choices and that the decisions made by empowered subordinates are better than those made by bosses who tell their subordinates what to do.

No process can always be the correct method, because different conditions lend themselves to different possibilities. A choice must be made as to what is feasible and most likely to be effective. During Entitlement and Fear, people's confidence and risk-taking ability are low. It isn't reasonable, then, to pursue empowerment as the work style. People who fear risk and lack confidence want to be told what to do and, frequently, how to do it. It is a waste of effort to ask people to be autonomous before they're confident.

Sometimes it's necessary to get upward feedback and engage in a dialogue with all of the constituencies. Sometimes that's not only unnecessary, it's undesirable. When time is of the essence, or there is no flexibility in what's to be done, or there's no real possibility of responding to the input—don't ask for feedback.

We need processes because without them, we'd be continually reinventing the wheel. But there is a danger when we allow processes to become elaborate. Elaborate processes make it easy to lose sight of the real goal. Worse, the more complex the process, the more it lends itself to becoming an Entitlement *solution*. Entitlement cultures create elaborate programs without serious regard to their outcome, because spending money is perceived as a solution. When the process becomes the point, it is not only ineffective, but also hugely expensive. An elaborate process becomes a pork barrel, a business unto itself, protected by those it feeds.

I became aware of this when I learned that the Wallace Company, an oil supply business in Texas that was the first winner of the Malcolm Baldrige Small Business Quality Award, went bankrupt and is no longer in business. Management said they had spent $2 million to develop their quality process, and they'd become so enamored of the process that they forgot to watch the business.

In the early 1990s I saw the write-in comments on an IBM internal survey. A very high percentage of people wrote in anger about IBM's effort to earn the Baldrige. They wrote things like, "Why are we doing this?" "We're investing millions of dollars and thousands of hours and for what?" "I don't see that this is getting us a better product or a faster delivery time!" And I saw many of my clients leaping on a process bandwagon, hiring staff, training the whole company, and pursuing process measurements that were unconnected to business outcomes.

I have become seriously alarmed at the techniques that many organizations are taking to increase their effectiveness or get into Earning. My largest concerns center around the tendency to identify human resources variables like empowerment, performance evaluation, ranking, compensation, or teamwork—or complex processes like continuous quality improvement or reengineering—and to create an elaborate program around the variable or process and expect that effort will get the organization into Earning.

An elaborate program centered around a human resources variable or a complex process rarely makes a significant difference in the business because usually the program—in-

stead of the business—has become the point. It's very dangerous that many of the people who create and run these programs sincerely believe they're moving the rock. It's even scarier
when you realize that if the program wasn't elaborate, neither
those directly involved nor anyone else would think the people
were doing a good job. The programs are like unbelievably
costly helium balloons that float on high, unconnected to what
really matters.

It's not a coincidence that there's been an extraordinary
proliferation of expensive and costly processes in the last decade. As they became popular, more people moved into the business of creating processes. Further, the more elaborate the
process, the greater the opportunity for people to have a career
by developing, teaching, and modifying it.

There's another reason why creating and running elaborate processes has become such a popular business. When people are scared and worried, working hard at a complex process
can give people the illusion that they know what to do when, in
fact, they don't. When you're in the Endless Danger Zone, it
can be very comforting to be preoccupied with the minutiae of
measurement and rules. Pursuing process acts as a psychological defense because it reduces feelings of uncertainty, confusion, dread, and powerlessness.

It's Entitlement when the goal is to create elaborate process. It's Fear when the motive is to cling to process as to a life
ring when the ship is going down. It's human to pursue a process rather than face up to the hard issues that require judgment.

15

Critical Conditions: Trust, Commitment, Success

The following critical conditions need to be created:

- *Trust in the Organization*
- *Clarity about Commitment*
- *Success*

Several years ago, the vice-president for finance of a company asked James Wetherbe, a management consultant, what he thought of Harry, the company's chief information officer. Harry reported to the vice-president of finance, who was disgusted with him. As far as the vice-president was concerned, Harry hadn't a clue as to what the vice-president wanted him to do.

Wetherbe met separately with both men. He asked Harry to create a list of what he believed were the ten most important things the vice-president wanted him to do, and he asked the vice-president to write down the ten most important things he wanted Harry to accomplish. Both men created perfectly reasonable lists, but their lists didn't match. Wetherbe showed Harry the list his boss had created.

Three months later the vice-president called Wetherbe to tell him he was a miracle worker. Harry, he observed, was now accomplishing everything he wanted done. He was so pleased he wanted Wetherbe to return and repeat whatever the magic process was with everyone else who reported to him.

Wetherbe told the vice-president there was no magic in the process. All he had done, he said, was to "show Harry your list." A long silence followed. Then the vice president said, "Well, that explains it. Harry's been cheating."

Wetherbe says that 80 percent of all of our apparent disagreements aren't disagreements; they're misunderstandings due to poor communication. He then uses this story as an example of the problems that are created by poor communication. But there is another way to interpret it. This story is not about misunderstanding and disagreement.

Trust in the Organization

That the vice-president hadn't communicated with Harry is a fact. *Why* hadn't he? He may be a power junkie who enjoys it when subordinates stand nervously on an uneven playing field, or he may be constantly testing Harry because he believes that if people really care about pleasing you, they'll know what you want. People do that all the time. For instance, "If you really loved me you'd have known what I wanted for my birthday."

Relationships that continuously test the parties involved generate conditions of mistrust. Ineffective communication creates mistrust. Core change characteristically creates mistrust.

Mistrust is costly. It creates paranoic conditions in which most of people's energies are used to protect themselves. Then, even when people are present, they are not *there*. Defensive and distracted, they are not psychologically available for purposeful actions. Therefore, in a competitive, borderless economy, *trust* has become a necessity.

Trust is a fundamental requirement for focused achievement, courageous decision making, creative disagreements, cooperation, teamwork, and a sense of unity. Trust is necessary to get people to buy in to new values and accept the process and consequences of change. A synergy of focus and effort relies on trust. No person and no organization can be in Earning without a core of trust. But the upheaval of major change always threatens trust because trust is based on predictability and consistency. Trust is created when people are told what's going to happen and it does. By definition, change creates unpredictability and inconsistency.

The perception of inconsistency is made worse when the people in control seem to lunge from one strategy to another, from one guru to the next, from one savior-process to the next program of the month. Instead of generating a sense of hope and trust, that kind of behavior increases people's cynicism about the wisdom and effectiveness of their leaders. Instead of responsive flexibility, this is perceived as the flailing about of desperate people.

The people at the top of the pyramid have to remember that an organization is like a pendulum. They're at the top of the pendulum, and blue- and pink-collar employees are at the bottom. When the pendulum swings, the top remains fixed while the bottom swings in the widest arc. Thus, people nearer the bottom are far more likely than people closer to the top to feel jerked around by things that are out of their control. Trust, therefore, is harder to create and sustain among that group.

It's always true that effective communication is both necessary and central to creating trust. A culture of either Fear or Entitlement acts as a barrier to that outcome. In Fear, few messages are sent, and no one "hears." Typically, there are few communications, because people either don't know what to say or they're afraid to tell the truth. Battered by anxiety and dread, besieged by rumors of unspeakable outcomes, listeners are cynical and mistrustful. Mentally, they're unable to *believe*. They don't believe people, and they don't believe what people say.

In Entitlement, there are many communications, but little is communicated. The process of communicating has become the point, and the point of the message is lost. The elaborateness of communications and their frequency make them ineffective. When the message is elaborated in three long articles and two hour-long videos, people will say, "I don't have time to get through that stuff." Then the stuff sits on shelves, unread and unwatched. We now have E-mail. It's become really easy to send messages to anyone and *everyone*. If you watch people reading their E-mail it's clear that most people just want to get through it rather than learn from it. IBM used to have television screens set up in all the buildings. They played IBM-internal programs and they were professional in quality. I never saw anyone, at any site, watching the screen.

Three conditions make it more difficult to communicate effectively: being in Entitlement, Fear, or the midst of major change. My colleague Norman Schoenfeld and I find that under those conditions, especially, it's necessary to:

1. Communicate much more simply and repetitiously than you think is necessary. Decide on the few main points that need to be made—try to limit them to five or less. While a full discussion can be held, the main thrust of a communication should be brief and simple. The same short and clear message needs to be repeated as many times as is necessary.

2. Never assume the message was received. When a message is sent, it's necessary to find out whether or not anyone heard anything, and if they did, what they believe was said. That allows you to learn if you need to repeat the message. Everyone is responsible for making sure they've communicated. They have an equal responsibility for being sure they've understood someone else's message. In general, don't ask people directly if they heard the message. If they didn't, they could become defensive. Instead, for example, if a change in policy was communicated, just ask people what they think of the new policy. That way you'll learn if they "heard." Then, restate what they said briefly and ask if that was correct. In that way, you'll find out if you "heard." Communication must necessarily be a two-way street.

3. Make most communications in person. In-person communications are usually significantly more effective than those by print, video, and electronics. The latter should be viewed as back-up communications, reinforcing the in-person message. Executives, managers, and leaders of all kind need to be visible, accessible, and aligned in terms of the messages they are sending. If the communication is made in a formal presentation, the message should not be read and the use of lots of overheads and slides should be avoided. Informal communications, such

as Hewlett-Packard's coffee talks where everybody gathers can be very effective.

4. Communicate, especially in-person, to explain any apparent inconsistency, ambiguity, and overlap in messages, programs, strategies, and goals. Inconsistency, ambiguity, and overlap reduce both trust and people's sense of confidence in the leadership.

5. Communicate successes. People's, team's, and unit's accomplishments need to be publicized and celebrated. Too often, management doesn't celebrate achievement, share good news, and reveal optimism about the future. That's self-defeating. If there's good news, shout it out!

6. Acknowledge difficulties and even failures. The tone of the message can still be positive in the sense that even negative experiences can teach us how to improve. Speak about hard times because if the topic is avoided and people learn about it, they will be convinced there's a hidden agenda. Hidden agendas absolutely preclude trust.

7. Remember that communicating effectively isn't always a matter of words. In the long run, what's done counts more than what's said. Specifically, executives and other leaders must walk the talk. They must do what they say. It's not okay for the leadership to freeze subordinate's wages and give themselves large bonuses when the company isn't making money. It's not walking the talk when the company has diversity programs and everyone with significant power is white and male. San Diego Gas and Electric didn't walk the talk when the executives said the organization would focus on customers and closed their print and graphics unit, which year after year had received the highest ratings in being customer focused. Not only is that not walking the talk, it's also a message to the whole organization that being the best at what's most important may not be good enough to save you. In general, that's a dangerous message to send.

Clarity About Commitment

About ten years ago I was a partner in the consulting firm Keilty, Goldsmith and Boone for a short while. The firm was expanding aggressively and continued to do so until about a year ago. That's when the senior partner, Dr. Marshall Goldsmith, told me, "Judy, I'm doing what you do, and I wish I'd done it a long time ago."

"Marshall," I said, "what exactly are you talking about?"

"I'm running a virtual corporation," he answered, "and I can't tell you how wonderful it is! When my people were employees, they kept asking for more. Now that everyone's an independent contractor, when I give them work, they all say thanks!"

A *virtual corporation* is a kind of organization in which there are very few or no permanent employees. Most self-employed people run virtual corporations. I have one full-time employee. The rest of the people who work with me are employed by the hour or project. While I may use the same people often and for many years, there is no commitment beyond that of the current task. That kind of arrangement is more common than is apparent, because the media don't usually address the working arrangements of the self-employed.

There is a spirited debate going on right now but it is definitely not out on the table. The issue is that of *commitment*. There is a competition in values between those who believe success requires the total freedom of a virtual corporation and those who are certain that success will always depend on employees who are committed to the organization, and therefore, the organization must make a commitment to its people.

One position says the future is and will continue to be unpredictable. And, since a borderless economy means neither nations nor organizations have unilateral control over what happens to them, organizations can't make long-term promises to anyone. If change is the constant, organizations must be flexible, continually ready to revise their vision and strategy. When there's no permanent or even long-term answer to the question, "What business are we in?" no organization can know for sure what skills will be critical even in the relatively short term. In this view, anyone who doesn't make a significant contribution could be laid off and should be. With this perspective, an organization maintains its right to have a labor force as continually flexible as its vision and strategy.*

The opposite view takes the position that success depends on people who are so motivated that, at least sometimes, they will put the organization's needs before their own. This position says that if organizations need commitment *from* their employees, they must make a commitment *to* their employees, because no one makes a commitment when a commitment is not made in return. Proponents of this position believe organizational competitiveness requires a mutual long-term partnership between employees and their organization, because that's the underpinning of employee involvement, trust, empowerment, teamwork, and lifelong learning.

The choice between being a virtual corporation or making some kind of commitment to employees is a profoundly philosophic decision as well as a logistic one. It answers the question of whether or not the employer elects to be concerned about people or chooses to be solely oriented to business.† If the choice is to be a virtual corporation, then issues of people's welfare don't limit decisions. If, on the other hand, the judgment is that the organization needs commitment from its employees, then the freedom of decision makers to act is limited by the need to consider the impact on employees. In that case, management would not be free to make decisions that jeopardized employee loyalty and trust.

A clear statement about commitment is especially necessary in those organizations that had a tradition of providing lifetime employment but elected to downsize with early retire-

*One outcome of this position is that, for the first time that I can remember, we're seeing performance evaluations that judge both the level of contribution and the value of the skill. People are being let go who are good performers but whose skills are no longer needed. In terms of employment security, that makes being a narrow specialist as dangerous as being a person with no specialty.

†In reality, things are not as clear as this. In the virtual corporations my friends and I run, we have terrific relationships with the people we employ. Those relationships develop naturally because we continuously select the people we work with. It's probably the case that the relationships have to be very good because the employer wants to be selected as much as the employee wants to be selected. But as employers, we do feel free to select and de-select people.

ment packages and layoffs. People need to know the rules of the new game. Without them, things appear illogical and inconsistent. Naturally, that increases people's feeling that their world is out of control and narcissistic expediency is the only survival strategy.

I have not yet seen employers step up to the issue directly. But they have to. All employers must be clear about the nature of the commitment they make to employees and the nature of the commitment they expect from employees. Obligations and expectations need to be overt and clear. Without clarity from the organization, people won't know where they stand, and they'll experience more anxiety than they should. Without a clear position, organizations will make inconsistent decisions that will fuel people's fears.

When security lay in the organization's commitment to lifetime security, the result was Entitlement and perpetual dependence, because there was inadequate risk. In 1994, three years after the 1990–1991 recession ended, many organizations have continued to downsize relentlessly because profitability has been achieved primarily by cutting costs. An obvious outcome is the old contract of mutual commitment, obligation, and loyalty is either in jeopardy, going, or gone. This condition, one in which the organization offers no way to earn security, is too scary for most people.

For the majority of people now, a commitment that would be seen as reasonable is one in which people would earn some form or some amount of security by achievement, predicated on the organization's ability to handle the costs of employment. In contrast to the absolute security that created Entitlement, this is *contingent security*, and it's based on the conditions of Earning. It would be a positive change that would encourage the development of confidence and courage. Contingent security is probably the condition most likely to develop people who will become genuinely comfortable in virtual corporations.

As the old contract is ending, we need a new one and it's very likely there will be several different versions. Some organizations already have different kinds of contracts, ranging from long-term employment to a contingency labor force. And some employers will choose to create a new contract of commitment, one in which there's no promise of lifetime employment, but there is a promise to keep employees marketable.

Today, the most commonly prescribed form of organizational commitment is that of providing employees with movable pensions, health benefits, and enough classroom education and job experience so that they are marketable. The idea is that if people's skills and knowledge are adequate and cutting-edge, even when they're no longer valuable to one employer, they will appeal to another or the skills will allow people to be self-employed.

While this position is put forth glibly, especially by the federal government, it's sufficiently costly to be controversial. A commitment to designing people's careers so that they remain current in knowledge in a range of tasks is a level of concern that organizations historically gave only to the first-track "best and brightest." Not everyone's career receives that kind of attention, because it's difficult and expensive. Training is a good investment, but it's also expensive. That's why IBM wants people to appreciate that they've been getting $2 billion worth of education a year.

If an employer needs to continuously lower costs in order to be competitive, it is hard to reconcile that with costly efforts to keep people marketable. The cost of keeping skills current continues to rise as the sophistication and complexity of the skills workers need to be employable has soared in recent years. For example, Citizen Utilities, a communications firm, says that high-tech communications systems will require workers who are trained in multiple functions. In addition to being expert in laying cable, they will also be expected to be skilled in marketing and able to work without supervision. The Baby Bell Nynex is planning a two-year technical course at the college level for workers, because workers have to be prepared to make decisions on their own. Rochester Telephone is increasing the salaries of employees who have cutting edge skills in both engineering and customer relations. Massachusetts General Hospital wants its computer specialists to know medical terms and be knowledgeable about hospital administration. Bank-America is having trouble finding systems engineers who can work in teams, because their people skills aren't nearly as well developed as their technical skills and the bank finds that unsatisfactory.

Most employees don't yet have the mindset that, literally, they are their own business. As they're unlikely to be lifetime employees of a single organization, no organization will be willing to take care of them. When lifetime employment was expected, employers accepted the paternalistic responsibility of making career, experiential, and educational decisions for their employees. That is ending, and it's a good thing. Very simply, people need to depend on themselves more and on organizations less.

Ray Smith, CEO of Bell Atlantic, said, "Once in the corporation, the employees own skills, talent, and personality must bring them to the fore, because the corporation isn't really tracking people." Bell Atlantic's training courses, he said, are now stored in the computers, and employees are responsible for learning what's available and mastering the content. Job openings are also listed in the computer, and employees are responsible for knowing what's available and applying for the position. Mostly, Smith said, employees are responsible for increasing their value to the company. There's nothing in Smith's message about taking care of employees. Being *taken care of* will not be part of the new commitment.

As it becomes an employee's responsibility to keep their skills up and to be visible as making a difference, they will have to accept more responsibility for themselves. They will need to make hard-nosed assessments of their value to the organization, of whether or not they fit in, and if they are accepted and respected.

People need to create initiatives in which they can demonstrate their value and they must strategize to make that happen. They need to make sure they have breadth and at least one area in depth. They need to position themselves so they're a key player, in the loop, in the business of the business. They have to become a person whose views are solicited and whose ideas are heard. This means that employees should try not to do work that doesn't give them a chance to learn or increase their visibility as people who make a difference. Employees need to be selective in accepting assignments that give them an opportunity to shine as individuals. Just when we're emphasizing team-work, the end of the old commitment of job security makes it imperative that people do work that allows them to say, "In 1994, I was responsible for gaining X number of customers, saving X number of dollars, increasing revenues by X." And everyone will have to seek out assignments that hone them on a hard stone, because everyone will have to be very sharp in an endlessly competitive employment situation.

All of this means that as security and paternalism end, em-ployees need to become much more selfish about where they work and what they do. People must become proactive and stra-tegic about their careers, the jobs they accept, and even the as-signments they take. To a far greater extent than before, their decisions need to be guided by whether or not the outcome will be good for them. This means that an increase in employee self-interest is necessary at the same time that organizations need a commitment to optimizing the good of the whole.

This apparent conflict is modulated by the reality that the individual's self-interests are best served if the organization is successful. Therefore, today's reality requires that people con-tribute to the welfare of the organization at the same time they are preparing themselves to leave, whether involuntarily in lay-offs or at their own initiative, to greater opportunity.

The new reality is work is a meritocracy. In a meritocracy, commitment is conditional on performance, and performance is always competitive. Coming from a culture of Entitlement, that's a change of revolutionary magnitude.

Success

Results of our questionnaire from an organization I was visiting revealed that the level of fear, dread, and anxiety was near par-alyzing levels. The image in the data was that of an organization run by leaders who were both tyrannical and floundering, un-certain of what to do, but whipping the troops hard.

Looking at the data and aware of the AMA Survey results, I asked, "Are you losing money?"

The general manager said, "No. We're making money."

Eighty-nine other managers in the room looked at him, obviously startled. Some called out, "We're not losing money?"

"No," he said. "We've made money every quarter. In fact, every quarter we've made more money than the last one."

No one else in the organization knew that. Because the general manager hoarded those results, everyone but him believed that their incredibly hard work was unsuccessful. Everyone believed they were losers in a losing organization.

Organizations must manage for *success*. Success is the only outcome that generates positive and purposeful energy; the sense of moving toward a future. Success is the only condition that generates the conviction, "We *can* do it!" Success is the only outcome that creates the light at the end of the tunnel, the conviction of a positive outcome, and the sense of cautious optimism in the midst of mega-change and uncertainty.

Everyone wants to be a winner in a winning organization. Nothing is as motivating as winning. And success is the only way that people develop confidence to handle risk and change. Therefore, the goal must always be to have as many individuals, teams, and business units earning success as possible.

Ideally, individuals, teams, and business units should be responsible for hitting *stretch targets,* targets which are difficult but achievable. Since the objective is to have as many people earning success as possible, the goal must be a real accomplishment, but it doesn't have to be Himalayan-high. It doesn't have to be a touchdown, a first down will suffice.

When the goals are hit, the accomplishment needs to be *celebrated!* I use that word rather than recognized or rewarded because I want to create a joyous image. The best organizations celebrate achievements as though they mean it. They give praise and awards gladly—"frequently, generously, publicly, personally, and passionately."

Celebration involves a generosity of spirit that one doesn't often see. In Fear, recognition rarely happens because there's too little joy to do something upbeat. In Entitlement, reward is buried in process. I remember a manager from First National Bank of Chicago who told me that when he asked the nomination committee to recognize his team, he was told he had missed the deadline. Process can kill the pleasure of rewards.

My firm was working with a successful unit of IBM, but morale wasn't high. People resented the fact that no matter what they accomplished, they didn't get recognized. That seemed an easy problem to solve. We told management they needed to recognize people more. The response was wholly negative: "We can't do that. By the time the nominating committee decides who will be recognized, no one remembers what they did and everyone else is ticked off, wondering why the other people got recognized and they didn't."

We told the managers the very best responses are heartfelt, personal, spontaneous, and real. "No," we were told, "you just don't get it." Actually, we did *get it* but we couldn't get them to give up the bureaucratic process and be spontaneous and joyful.

We were more successful with a manager from AT&T. She said, "Now I understand a remark that was made to me. I was on the banquet committee. We arranged the banquet for the people the nominating committee wanted recognized. I was standing at the door of the dining room, and one of the people being recognized said to me, 'You know, I'd have appreciated a thirty-second phone call from the vice-president a hell of a lot more than this.'" Ritual recognition often isn't a celebration.

The AT&T manager continued: "Now I understand the power of what our boss did last week. He never did anything like it before. He called everyone to the cafeteria. That's the only room we have large enough to hold everybody. He said, 'As you all know, we've been writing competitive bids. It's a real pleasure for me to tell you that we've landed three! Now I'm going to call out the names of the people on the winning teams.' He did that and they all stepped forward. As the names were called, we got more and more excited. We were clapping and whistling! What a great moment! Next to that, the banquet was nothing."

One of the great examples of an organization that really knows how to celebrate is Mary Kay Cosmetics. In 1993, thirty-six thousand Mary Kay consultants, their term for saleswomen, converged on Dallas for a three-day sales rally that was probably the greatest women's party on earth. The consultants got kissed by Mary Kay and cheered by thousands. Depending on how much they sold, they received a rose, a crown, a diamond ring, even a pink Cadillac. That organization recognizes people! It's a party and it's joyous. They *celebrate* each other's success with a generosity of heart. That's the model.

There's a very significant difference between managing for success and managing for morale. The great majority of organizations I deal with manage for morale. That includes surveys in which many of the questions begin with *Are you satisfied?* "Are you satisfied with your pay? With your working conditions? How you're treated? Do you *like* your manager?" These are very different questions from, "Are your goals stretch targets? Can you *earn* more responsibility? Are you *accomplishing* more than you thought you could? Do you *respect* your manager?"

Managing for morale is dangerous because it can reinforce Entitlement. Instead, organizations must manage for success. Morale naturally reaches its highest levels where there is success.

But to be effective, you must understand the difference between business and psychological success. My colleague Norman Schoenfeld is a pragmatic business man. He and I were having dinner after a day of interviewing people in a unit of Hewlett-Packard. Norm suddenly put his fork down, looked at me and asked, "Why do we bother with this stuff?"

I blurted out, "If there's no psychological success you're not going to have sustained business success."

The business unit we were studying was financially successful. But executives at a higher level than the unit refused to let the unit grow. As orders piled in, people had to work extraordinarily long hours because there were too few employees. In fact, there had been a downsizing shortly before orders exploded. The profits generated by the unit were used either to shore up other units with poor results or to make investments in other parts of the business. From white to blue collar, the employees in the unit *understood* the reasons for the business strategy but they *felt* bitter.

Business success (profitability, market share, or stock price) is a necessary but not sufficient condition for creating *psychological success* (motivation, enthusiasm, and commitment). Psychological success requires a positive outcome for the people who created the business success. Both kinds of success are necessary for sustained high levels of morale (see Figure 15-1).

It must not be assumed that business success will create psychological success. Instead, it must be determined whether or not the people who achieve the targets benefited from the success they create. If there's no personal experience of gaining as a result of the business success, over time, the outcome is likely to be psychological failure (demotivation, mistrust, and cynicism). Then, naturally enough, people are less willing to put the organization's needs before their own, and they're less willing to work very hard. Instead, they ask, "What's in this for me?"

Psychological success is a prerequisite for sustained business success. It's a necessity and not a luxury, because without it, there's no emotional commitment to the organization, its mission, or its leaders. Without psychological success, management can create a surge in effort and productivity, but it won't be sustained. Sustained motivation, effort, and enthusiasm requires the emotional commitment that comes from psychological success. Again: Celebrate!

- Sustained business success requires psychological success.

Figure 15-1. The relationship between psychological and business success.

Business Success		Psychological Success	
		Low	High
High		Attila the Hun: Possible for the short term	Touchdown! Way to go!
Low		The Gulag: A real downer	Warm and fuzzy flop: Unsustainable good feelings

- Short-term psychological success is possible without business success.
- Long-term psychological success rests on business success.
- Prolonged business failure will create psychological failure.

16

Give Thanks for Hard Times

Failure is unsettling and, in that sense, is the stick (and not the carrot). But a crisis can also be an unfreezing process that by itself creates change. In that sense it is also opportunity.

Organizations often overlook the potential for good in the urgency created by failure. When expensive disappointments create a sense of crisis, the urgency can be harnessed as a significant lever for change.

In truth, it's usually failure, disappointment, and frustration that motivate people to reexamine that which they've taken for granted. It's rare to find big change without significant bad news. It's only when the old ways of doing things are clearly not working that the path is cleared for new ways to be introduced. After all, if the old ways continue to generate success, it's immensely difficult to argue successfully for change. In that sense, the pain of failure creates the largest opportunities for progress.

When times are scary, it's hard to feel optimistic. Big changes are usually frightening. But in the long run, stepping up to change and dealing with it usually has positive outcomes. The written Chinese word for *crisis* consists of two symbols: one meaning *hard times* and the other *opportunity*.

Coping with Mega-Change

In the last few years I've observed four reasonably predictable phases that people and organizations go through as they cope with mega-change:

Phase 1. The first response is to not perceive the change. No one wants to see that reality has changed enormously because that's fundamentally scary. It means the knowledge gained in the past will probably be irrelevant or ineffective, because the present is fundamentally different from the past.

The first phase of dealing with quantum change is to ignore it. Explanations are put forth about why things aren't working as well as they did before, within a cognitive structure in which nothing fundamental has altered. The reasons that are offered are logical and plausible—if the present was like the past. You might hear, for example, "Mainframe computer sales are down because there's a recession in Europe and Japan."

Phase 2. The second phase occurs when the recession is over and sales have still not increased significantly. Now, the explanations are that "We aren't doing *it* hard enough." The second phase involves buckling down. The organization then does what it used to, but harder, faster, and sometimes with more people. Coping is still imagined within the structure of the past. Now you might hear, "Mainframe sales are still down, but we're putting all of our people through an extra week of training. We're also changing their compensation. Are they going to be motivated!"

It is only after these efforts fail that people allow themselves to see that conditions truly different from what they were. The present is not like the past, and they have to do very different things.

Phase 3. During the third phase, there are typically several years during which there's a lot of flailing around. They know they can't continue as they were, but they don't know what to do. Understandably, that's often a bleak period, a period of frustration.

In this phase nothing terribly good happens, there's no

major breakthrough to something positive. People have to get past the extremes of negative emotions—of fear, anxiety, and depression—before they begin to perceive opportunity. As these emotions moderate with time and the mega-changes no longer seem so foreign, people begin to discern small points of light in what had seemed to be a black tunnel.

Phase 4. In the fourth phase, people begin to perceive new opportunities. The fact that success eluded them no matter how hard they tried is what brings them into a future that's different. Now one might hear, "Our new chip is a real breakthrough. We can organize parallel processors and give our customers mainframe capacity at half the old price. What a marketing opportunity!"

The organizations which move into phase four are *en route* to the success of growth. That growth would not have been achieved if they hadn't been forced by failure and frustration to perceive the need for major internal change. Like people, many corporations have to hit bottom before they can achieve success.

The United States, Europe, and Japan

Although it continues to be painful, the best thing that happened to the United States was our rude awakening when forced out of Entitlement, because we were losing in the borderless economy. American corporations responded years before their counterparts in Japan and Europe. Business in the United states began the journey from Entitlement through Fear to Earning while employees, managers, unions, and governments in Europe and Japan remained in Entitlement by refusing to perceive the new reality.

Europe is just emerging from its worst recession since World War II. Its businesses are experiencing increasing pressure from global competition. Its executives need to cut costs aggressively to counteract their declining competitiveness in the world's markets. But cutting costs is extremely difficult because of the high potential for widespread labor strife in the face of soaring job insecurity and unemployment. Edward Moerk, president of Campbell Biscuits Europe said, "This is the dying of the dinosaurs. I just cannot see anybody realistically believing that what we are going through in Europe is a recession. What we are going through is an economic restructuring. Europe is no longer competitive."

In Japan, pessimism is prevalent. The fact that the American economy is growing at least 3 percent, significantly faster than Japan's 1 percent or less, is becoming an obsession. Symbols of Japan's economic miracle—politicians trashing American workers or rising suns obliterating American flags—have essentially disappeared. Instead, headlines declare the United States is a "rising Sam." Japanese manufacturers who were protected from foreign competition have become less innovative and competitive.

To a very great extent, the corporations and governments of both Europe and Japan have been reluctant to break the tradition of employee protection or Entitlement. As a result, they're losing ground in cost and creativity. In a borderless economy, continued Entitlement destroys competitiveness.

In many European countries the combined costs of payroll taxes and employer contributions to pensions, unemployment, and other benefits amounts to over 50 percent of the cost of wages. In the United States that figure is 19.3 percent. EU policy makers are studying how their economies can become more flexible, but those changes necessarily involve reducing costs and regulations. These changes are likely to involve cutting back on the welfare state that characterizes those countries.

Not surprisingly, efforts at reducing entitlements always provoke resistance to change by those with a psychology of Entitlement. Europe's labor leaders are determined not to give up the rights that labor won. But the conditions that created those gains *as rights* are over. In the face of slow growth in their economies and in the number of jobs, more Europeans are being forced to realize their economic systems and their generosity cannot be continued.

While continued downsizing and some unemployment—especially among professionals and managers—means there is still some pain and fear, the aggregate productivity figures for

American business is rising sharply. That's not true in Japan or Europe. This is a development of "transcendent importance."

A study of American, Japanese, and European businesses from 1987 to 1992 in globally competitive industries shows clearly that the Americans have won in the competition. The Americans captured 37 percent of sales and 48 percent of the profits in global markets. In *The Wall Street Journal*, David Strickberger commented, "In this sense the United States had produced something close to the trade version of olympic basketball's dream team."

Demonstrating the triumph of the free market, Strickberger finds that American industry is either the leader or is very competitive in virtually every major global industry. In technologically intensive industries, American companies are the leaders in computers, software, and data processing; electronic equipment; electrical components; and health care, including pharmaceuticals. Americans also lead in food, beverages, tobacco, and personal care. U.S. companies have given up market share in industries with low profits, and they have leapfrogged over their rivals as they moved into the lead in high-profit businesses.

In addition, though it's not like the glory decades following World War II, American industry is creating jobs at a much higher rate than industries in Japan and Europe. In the past decade, the United States created over 18 million net new jobs. Despite a population larger than that of the United States and twice that of Japan, Europe generated 6.9 million jobs. In the same time period, Japan created 8 million new jobs. As a result of the recession, there has been a slowdown in job growth in Japan. Estimates are that Europe will experience a net decline in positions between 1944–96. The United States created more than one million new jobs in 1993.

The American economy is closer to that process economist Schumpeter called "creative destruction" than are the economies of Europe and Japan. Relatively speaking, we are less prone to support expensive government social welfare programs, and we are more willing to give individual businesses the freedom to make hard choices. Thus, downsizing is harsher here, and even large and profitable companies are continuing to lay off large numbers of people. But at the same time, other organizations with greater growth potential prosper, grow, and create jobs.

While it cannot be totally unbridled, overall the free market is ultimately the only efficient and effective governor of an economy. The outcome of the pain of losing the Comfort Zone and struggling through Fear has been positive. The present and the future require being in Earning. Thus, in the last year, I have become cautiously optimistic.

No one ever says, "Thanks for giving me a hard time." But they should. It's only when we have to cope with really hard times that we deliver at levels of accomplishment we didn't know we could reach. The Danger Zone is permanent. Being in the Danger Zone will force us to continue to focus on what really matters while we perform at the highest levels we can. It's only when we have to meet continuous challenge that we develop the skills and the conviction that we *can* deal with anything life throws our way. What a great outcome that is! So, remember to:

Move the rock!
Manage to Success!
And give thanks for hard times!

Notes on Sources

The source citations are keyed to the text by page number and a short phrase in boldface type.

Chapter 1

Page

12   **Committee to Allocate Office Space:** Judith M. Bardwick, *The Plateauing Trap.* New York: AMACOM, 1986.

13   **". . . while getting ahead":** Nancy Gibbs, "How America Has Run Out of Time," *Time* (April 24, 1989), pp. 58–67. Quotation from page 60.

13   **". . . for their children":** "Special Report. Warning: The Standard of Living is Slipping," *Business Week* (April 20, 1987), pp. 48–52.

13   **". . . outlook—all bad":** James C. Cooper and Kathleen Madigan, "Business Outlook; Desperately Seeking a Dose of Productivity," *Business Week* (February 19, 1990), p. 27.

14   **rate of 0.9 percent in the 1980s:** Vivian Brownstein, "New Threats to the Expansion," *Fortune* (July 25, 1994), pp. 56–64.

14   **productivity increases since mid-1990:** Robert J. Samuelson, "Reinventing Corporate America," *Newsweek* (July 4, 1994), p. 53.

14   **security is the customer:** Erroll B. Davis, Jr., president, Wisconsin Power and Light, personal communication, 1989.

14   **". . . a deck chair on the *Titanic*":** Daniel Machalaba, "Building Steam. Union Pacific Changes Its Hidebound Ways Under

New Chairman," *The Wall Street Journal* (January 18, 1989), pp. 1, 9. Reprinted by permission of *The Wall Street Journal,* © 1989, Dow Jones & Company, Inc. All Rights Reserved Worldwide.

15 **cut from the corporate ranks:** L. M. Applegate, J. I. Cash, Jr., and D. Q. Mills, "Information Technology and Tomorrow's Manager," *Harvard Business Review* (November-December 1988), pp. 128–136.

15 **as high as 2 million:** J. H. McKerring, "An Assessment of the Role That Outplacement Services Play in Addressing the Negative Psychological Impact Experienced Through Mid-Career Job Loss," unpublished thesis, University of San Francisco, September 1988.

15 **at twice the 1989 rate:** Michael J. Mandel, "This Time, the Downturn Is Dressed in Pinstripes," *Business Week* (October 1, 1990), pp. 130–131.

15 **in the early 1990s:** Ron Zemke, "Putting the SQUEEZE on Middle Managers," *Training* (December 1988), pp. 41–46.

16 **and Texaco Incorporated:** Christopher Byron, "The Big Hurt," *New York* (October 18, 1993), p. 26.

16 **to 11,546,647:** Richard S. Teitelbaum, "Hats Off! It Was a Heck of a Year," *Fortune* (April 18, 1994), pp. 210–217.

16 **the expense of job security:** G. Pascal Zachery and Bob Ortega, "Workplace Revolution Boosts Productivity at Cost of Job Security," *The Wall Street Journal* (March 10, 1993), pp. A1, A8.

16 **management in the preceding year:** Families and Work Institute, *National Study of the Changing Workforce,* 1993.

16 **employed 16,735,000 people:** J. Wolf, "Career Plateauing in the Public Service: Baby Boom and Employment Bust," *Public Management Forum* (March/April 1983), pp. 160–165.

17 **computer networks and data bases:** Howard Gleckman, John Carey, Rusell Mitchell, Tim Smart, Chris Roush, and bureau reports, "The Technology Payoff," *Business Week* (June 14, 1993), pp. 57–65.

17 **studied productivity in the service sector:** Howard Banks, "What's Ahead for Business," *Forbes* (April 11, 1994), p. 41.

17 **despite the strength of our economy:** R. M. Tomasko, *Downsizing.* New York: AMACOM, 1987.

18 **"... You are Family"**: Amanda Bennett, "Broken Bonds," *The Wall Street Journal,* December 8, 1989, p. R21. Reprinted by permission of *The Wall Street Journal,* © 1989, Dow Jones & Company, Inc. All Rights Reserved Worldwide.

Chapter 2

Page

24 **if the employer loses.** John Hoerr, "Needed: A Replacement for the Bargaining Table," *Business Week* (January 9, 1989), pp. 38–39.

25 **30,000 pages of regulations:** Norman R. Augustine, "Defense: A Case of Too Many Cooks," *Fortune* (December 5, 1988), pp. 219–220.

25 **7 pages for pencils:** Howard Banks, ed., "What's Ahead for Business," *Forbes* (February 19, 1990), p. 33.

25 **1,200 pages long:** Julie A. Lopez, "Bucking Tradition," *The Wall Street Journal* (March 15, 1989), pp. 1, 8. Reprinted by permission of *The Wall Street Journal,* © 1989, Dow Jones & Company, Inc. All Rights Reserved Worldwide.

26 **"... a hole in the wall":** Stratford P. Sherman, "The Mind of Jack Welch," *Fortune* (March 27, 1989), pp. 39–50. Quotation from p. 46.

Chapter 3

Page

35 **eliminated back in 1987:** Joseph B. White and Neal Templin, "Auto Pact Leaves GM Hard Choice: Go Along or Confront in the Union," *The Wall Street Journal* (September 17, 1993), pp. A1, A4.

35 **they've been in the new job:** *New York Times,* excerpted in "GM Offers Paid-But-Idle Workers Up to $60,000 to Move to Four Plants," *San Jose Mercury News* (June 25, 1994), p. 14C.

36 **That's my world:** Joshua Hyatt, "The Last Shift," *Inc.* (February 1989), pp. 74–80. Reprinted with permission, *Inc.* Magazine (February 1989). Copyright © 1989, by Goldhirsh Group, Inc., 38 Commercial Wharf, Boston, Mass. 02110.

36   **". . . lose your job tomorrow":** Restaino Baker, Schumann &
        Co., Marketing Research, "Final Report on Focus Groups" (of
        a utility company), January 1989.

36   **companies cut their payrolls:** Ronald Henkoff, "Cost Cut-
        ting: How to Do It Right," *Fortune* (April 9, 1990), pp. 40–49.
        AMA surveys 1987–1990 on p. 40. 1990 AMA Survey on
        downsizing, "Summary of Key Findings," is now available.

37   **maintain profits and markets:** Ron Zemke, "The Ups and
        Downs of Downsizing," *Training* (November 1990), pp. 27–34.

38   **going on around them:** Ibid.

39   **". . . afraid to take risks":** Henkoff, pp. 40, 41.

39   **rate of 2.5 percent annually:** Sherman, pp. 39–50.

39   **or $2.1 million:** Anne B. Fisher, "The Downside of Downsiz-
        ing," *Fortune* (May 23, 1988), pp. 42–52. Quotation from
        p. 42.

39   **deteriorated after the layoffs:** Henkoff, p. 40.

40   **surviving employees to take risks:** John A. Byrne, "There Is
        an Upside to Downsizing," *Business Week* (May 9, 1994), pp.
        60–69. The quotation is from page 68.

40   **". . . I can trust you":** "When Employees Speak, AT&T Lis-
        tens," *Focus* (December 15, 1987), pp. 4–7.

42   **back to worrying again:** Fisher, p. 42.

43   **substance of real work:** Abraham Zaleznik, "Real Work," *Har-
        vard Business Review* (January-February 1989), pp. 57–64.
        Quotation from p. 60.

43   **their own work unit:** Hal Burlingame, HWB Planning Con-
        ference, Revision (October 27, 1987).

44   **". . . and cooperation among departments":** Tom Thomas,
        "Employees Strongly Committed, Unsure About Future,"
        PG&E Week (August 14, 1987), pp. 1–3. Quotation from p. 3.

44   **they won't share information:** Walter Kiechel III, "How Im-
        portant Is Morale, Really?" *Fortune* (February 13, 1989), pp.
        121–122.

44   **". . . 'It's mine, all mine' ":** Jacob M. Schlesinger and Paul
        Ingrassia, "People Power: GM Woos Employees by Listening
        to Them, Talking of Its 'Team,' " *The Wall Street Journal* (Jan-
        uary 12, 1989), pp. 1, 7. Quotation from p. 1. Reprinted by

permission of *The Wall Street Journal,* © 1989, Dow Jones & Company, Inc. All Rights Reserved Worldwide.

51 **". . . of his subordinate's endurance":** Peter Nulty, "America's Toughest Bosses," *Fortune* (February 27, 1989), pp. 40–54. Quotation from p. 54.

Chapter 4

Page

58 **good of the whole:** Ted Levitt, "From the Editor; Decisions," *Harvard Business Review,* Reprint 89115.

62 **grit and self-control:** Robert E. Kelley, "In Praise of Followers," *Harvard Business Review* (November-December 1988), pp. 142–148.

62 **". . . it's a competitive necessity":** Stratford P. Sherman, "The Mind of Jack Welch," *Fortune* (March 27, 1989), pp. 39–50. Quotation from p. 46.

62–
63 **rewards people who excel:** William Taylor, "The Business of Innovation: An Interview with Paul Cook," *Harvard Business Review* (March-April 1990), pp. 97–106. Quotation from pp. 99–100.

Chapter 5

Page

65 **". . . of anxiety are attained":** Donald Norfolk, *Executive Stress.* New York: Warner Books, 1989. Quotation from p. 12.

65 **uncertainty) reaches 50 percent:** John W. Atkinson, "Motivational Determinants of Risk Taking Behavior," *Psychological Review,* vol. 64, no. 6, 1957, p. 365.

Chapter 6

Page

86–
87 **". . . and provide greater incentives":** Whitman quoted in

Thomas A. Stewart, "CEOs See Clout Shifting," *Fortune* (November 6, 1989), p. 66.

88 **at half the cost:** Ronald Henkoff, "Cost Cutting: How to Do It Right," *Fortune* (April 9, 1990), pp. 40–49.

88–
89 **creating a horizontal organization:** Lori Bongiorno, Therese Palmer, Judy Temes, and bureau reports, "The Horizontal Corporation," *Business Week* (December 20, 1993), pp. 76–83.

93 **absentees are swiftly noticed:** Louis Kraar, "Japan's Gung-Ho U.S. Car Plants," *Fortune* (January 30, 1989), pp. 98–108.

93 **the car might be like:** Kim B. Clark and Takahiro Fujimoto, "The Power of Product Integrity," *Harvard Business Review* (November-December 1990), pp. 107–118.

94 **for contribution, not status:** Edward E. Lawler III, "Putting It All Together," unpublished manuscript. 19 pages.

95 **". . . to reflect this shortfall":** Jaclyn Fierman, "The Perilous New World of Far Pay," *Fortune* (July 13, 1994), pp. 57–64.

95 **increase productivity became clear:** Nancy J. Perry, "Here Come Richer, Riskier Pay Plans," *Fortune* (December 19, 1988), pp. 50–58.

95 **positive results in any era:** Linda Stockman Vines, "Creative Compensation Strategies," *Solutions* (January 1994), pp. 22–26.

95 **production and financial goals:** Gilbert Fuchsberg, "Managing," *The Wall Street Journal* (April 30, 1990), p. B1. Reprinted by permission of *The Wall Street Journal,* © 1990, Dow Jones & Company, Inc. All Rights Reserved Worldwide.

96 **". . . what was in it for us":** Fierman, p. 63.

96 **100 percent of their salary:** "Here Comes GM's Saturn," *Business Week* (April 9, 1990), p. 59.

96 **". . . a tool to drive results":** Fuchsberg, p. B1.

96 **more responsibility and autonomy:** Alan S. Blinder, "Want to Boost Productivity? Try Giving Workers a Say," *Business Week* (April 17, 1989), p. 10.

97 **relation to company performance:** Graef S. Crystal, "Where's the Risk in CEO's Rewards?" *Fortune* (December 19, 1988), pp. 62–66.

99 **General Electric, and Westinghouse:** Henkoff, p. 48.

Chapter 7

Page

106 **". . . what you're going to do":** Brian Dumaine, "The New Turnaround Champs," *Fortune* (July 16, 1990), p. 39.

112 **off to go to school:** Michael Brody, "Helping Workers to Work Smarter," *Fortune* (June 8, 1987), pp. 85–88.

112 **on a shared salary basis:** John Neuman, "What to Know Before Trying Japanese Ideas . . ." *Boardroom Reports* (January 15, 1989), p. 5.

Chapter 8

Page

119 **". . . but never vigorously pursued":** Michael E. Porter, "The Competitive Advantage of Nations," *Harvard Business Review* (March-April, 1990), pp. 73–93. Quotation from p. 74. Reprinted by permission of the *Harvard Business Review*. Copyright © 1990 by the President and Fellows of Harvard College; all rights reserved.

124 **opportunities to learn something:** J. Sterling Livingston, "Pygmalion in Management," *Harvard Business Review* (September-October 1988), pp. 121–130. Shaw quotation from p. 121.

124 **questions from the audience:** "New Organization Will Be Quicker to Respond to Customer Needs, *Update Spotlight* (August 27, 1990), vol. 13, no. 31, special edition of the newsletter of Pacific Bell, p. 3.

128 **Waterman calls "directed autonomy":** Robert H. Waterman, *The Renewal Factor: How the Best Get and Keep the Competitive Edge.* New York: Bantam, 1987.

129 **life will improve dramatically:** Noel Tichy and Ram Charan, "Speed, Simplicity, Self-Confidence: An Interview with Jack Welch," *Harvard Business Review* (September-October 1989), pp. 112–120. Quotation from p. 118.

130 **". . . as responsibility and authority":** Thomas A. Stewart, "New Ways to Exercise Power," *Fortune* (November 6, 1989), pp. 52–64. Quotation from p. 52.

130   **". . . to do things than you are":** Ibid., p. 54.

131   **contributed to the company:** Jay W. Lorsch and Haruo Ta-
        kagi, "Keeping Managers off the Shelf," *Harvard Business Re-
        view* (July-August 1986), pp. 60–65.

132   **a worker named Hwang:** Ira Magaziner and Mark Patinkin,
        "Fast Heat: How Korea Won the Microwave War," *Harvard
        Business Review* (January-February 1989), pp. 83–92. Quota-
        tion from p. 90.

133   **". . . I do a little tap dance":** Adam Smith, "The Modest Bil-
        lionaire," *Esquire* (October 1988), pp. 103–108. Quotation
        from p. 108.

Chapter 9

Page

134–

135   **Japan's was 81 percent:** Howard Banks, "What the Gloom-
        Mongers Overlook," *Forbes* (October 2, 1989), p. 37, 54.

135   **called a "bureaucratic behemoth":** Pat Baldwin, "Focusing
        on the Big Picture," *American Way* (July 1, 1989), pp. 40–44.
        Quotation from p. 40.

135   **that included more layoffs:** Associated Press, "Wall Street Fo-
        cuses on Woes at Kodak," *The San Diego Union* (July 4, 1989),
        section D, pp. 1, 2.

136   **to more than 46 percent:** Seth Lubove, "Aim, Focus, and
        Shoot," *Forbes* (November 26, 1990), p. 67.

136   **". . . have to do it all over again":** Associated Press, p. 1.

136   **as a paternalistic caretaker:** Keith H. Hammonds, "A Mo-
        ment Kodak Wants to Capture," *Business Week* (August 27,
        1990), pp. 52–53.

136   **". . . this is somewhat paternalistic":** Associated Press, p. 2.

136   **over as chairman and CEO:** Lubove, p. 67.

137   **people are controlling themselves:** Thomas A. Stewart, "New
        Ways to Exercise Power," *Fortune* (November 6, 1989), pp. 52–
        64. Quotation from p. 52.

137   **". . . problem, and then go away":** William Taylor, "The Gray
        Area," *Harvard Business Review* (January-February 1989), pp.
        178–180. Quotation from p. 180.

138–
139   **IBM's Guiding Principles:** From IBM Managers' Manual, Preface, Index/Page: MM-02.1, Issued 3/16/89.

140   **large organizations take eight to ten:** Jack E. Bowsher, *Educating America*. New York: John Wiley, 1989.

141   **give people a new role:** Michael Beer, Russell A. Eisenstat, and Bert Spector, "Why Change Programs Don't Produce Change," *Harvard Business Review* (November-December 1990), pp. 158–166.

142   **". . . environment in which we do business":** Speech delivered at meeting of Wisconsin Power and Light, Green Lake, Wisconsin, September 1, 1987.

146   **and of better quality:** Charles C. Manx and Henry P. Sims, Jr., *Superleadership*. New York: Prentice-Hall, 1989, p. 179. Reprinted by permission of the publisher, Prentice-Hall Press, a division of Simon & Schuster, New York, New York.

147   **". . . to see things work differently":** Manx and Sims, p. 175. Reprinted by permission of the publisher, Prentice-Hall, a division of Simon & Schuster, New York, New York.

147   **the highly successful Taurus:** Ibid. Reprinted by permission of the publisher, Prentice-Hall, a division of Simon & Schuster, New York, New York.

147   **in the first quarter of 1991:** Joseph B. White, "Big Three Auto Makers' Quarterly Loss Could Total $3 Billion, Analysts Believe," *The Wall Street Journal* (March 4, 1991), p. A4.

147   **Subaru, Isuzu, and Mazda:** Joseph B. White, Krystal Miller, and Robert L. Simison, "GM and Ford Post First-Quarter Deficits, Are Expected to Be Unprofitable for '91," *The Wall Street Journal* (May 1, 1991), p. A3.

148   **primary cause of the recession:** James C. Cooper and Kathleen Madigan, "A Quick Economic Recovery? Don't Bet the Ranch," *Business Week* (February 25, 1991), p. 27.

148   **they can't get financing:** David Wessel and Paul Duke, Jr., "Greenspan Still Expects Upturn: Car Sales Aren't Liberated by Peace," *The Wall Street Journal* (March 14, 1991), p. A2.

148   **are predicted for 1991:** Henry F. Myers, "An Anemic Recovery May Be Very Healthy," *The Wall Street Journal* (March 11, 1991), p. A1.

148 **Real incomes are declining:** James C. Cooper and Kathleen Madigan, "Empty Pockets Are Still Keeping Recovery on Hold," *Business Week* (March 18, 1991), p. 25.

151 **It could even fall:** Ronald Henkoff, "Make Your Office More Productive," *Fortune*, February 25, 1991, pp. 72–84.

151 **Management is also simplifying:** First discussed in Judith M. Bardwick, "Escaping the Plateauing Trap: Advice for Individuals and Organizations," *New Jersey Bell Journal*, vol. 10, no. 2, Summer 1987, pp. 1–12.

Chapter 10

Page

154 **of stocks and bonds:** Adam Smith, "The Modest Billionaire," Esquire (October 1988), pp. 103–108.

Chapter 11

Page

171 **saving $52 million a year:** Alex Taylor III, "The Tasks Facing General Motors," *Fortune* (March 13, 1989), pp. 52–59.

173 **". . . terms of real creativity":** Stephen K. Yoder, "Japan's Scientists Find Pure Research Suffers Under Rigid Life Style," *The Wall Street Journal* (October 31, 1988), pp. A1, A5. Reprinted by permission of *The Wall Street Journal,* © 1988, Dow Jones & Company, Inc. All Rights Reserved Worldwide.

173 **". . . in which we operate":** Patricia McCracken, "In the Cause of Change," *ThinkTwice* (December 1993), p. 16.

180 **the previous conventional one:** Saul W. Gellerman and William A. Hodgson, "Cyanamid's New Take on Performance Appraisal," *Harvard Business Review* (May-June 1988), pp. 36–41.

Chapter 12

Page

186 **their old jobs are gone forever:** G. Pascal Zachary and Bob Ortega, "Age of Angst: Workplace Revolution Boosts Produc-

tivity at Cost of Job Security," *The Wall Street Journal* (March 10, 1993), pp. A1, A8.

188 **the model I put forth in this book:** Eric Rolfe Greenberg, ed., "Survey: Increased Comfort, Decreased Profits," *HR focus,* American Management Association's Conference Daily (April 15, 1992); Eric Rolfe Greenberg, ed., *Survey Results,* American Management Association Seminar-By-Satellite Professional Secretaries Day (April 22, 1992).

191 **". . . not by a long shot":** Laurie Hays, "Blue Period," *The Wall Street Journal* (May 13, 1994), pp. A1, A8.

Chapter 13

Page

194 **". . . a little hungry and a little scared":** Kerry Pechter, "Rebooting Big Blue," *Human Resource Executive* (September 1993), pp. 1, 23.

195 **"The answer to morale is action":** David Kirkpatrick, "Lou Gerstner's First 30 Days," *Fortune* (May 31, 1993), pp. 57–62.

195 **". . . we shall never surrender":** Winston Churchill, speech on Dunkirk, House of Commons (June 4, 1940).

196 **gaining a strategic advantage:** Michael Treacy, "A Better Deal Every Year," *The Index SMI Review* (Fourth Quarter 1993), pp. 3–6.

198 **or it would be gone:** Pechter, pp. 1, 23.

198 **as to how the corporation did:** Gilbert Fuschberg, "Why Shake-Ups Work for Some, Not for Others," *The Wall Street Journal* (October 1, 1993), p. B1.

198 **". . . managers should lose":** Russell Mitchell, "Safeway's Low-Fat Diet," *Business Week* (October 18, 1993), pp. 60–61.

198 **set aside for variable pay:** Pechter, pp. 1, 23.

201 **". . . Leave the meeting":** Kirkpatrick, pp. 57–62.

201 **20 percent of the reengineering efforts:** David Robinson, "Overcoming the Odds," *Index SMI Review* (Fourth Quarter 1993), pp. 11–13.

Chapter 14

Page

203   **". . . they all have their own agenda":** "Now Hear This," *Fortune* (February 7, 1994), p. 20.

203   **models of buildings on the campus:** Joseph Pereira, "The Red Block Is From My Pile. Is Not. Is Too. Is Not. Is Too." *The Wall Street Journal* (July 12, 1994), p. B1.

204   **fell entirely within their functional responsibility:** Raymond W. Smith, "Managing Change and HR: A CEO's Perspective," Human Resource Conference, Sanibel Island, Florida (October 4, 1993).

Chapter 15

Page

213   **the company's chief information officer:** James Wetherbe, "How to Be a Master Communicator," *Index SMI Review* (Fourth Quarter, 1993), pp. 17–19.

214   **". . . Harry's been cheating":** Ibid, p. 18.

221   **costly to be controversial:** Department of Labor Proposal: Workforce Security Act of 1993.

221   **$2 billion worth of education a year:** Pechter, pp. 1, 23.

221   **who are trained in multiple functions:** Albert R. Karr, "Labor Letter," *The Wall Street Journal* (July 19, 1994), p. A1.

222   **". . . corporation isn't really tracking people":** Smith.

224   **". . . publicly, personally, and passionately":** Norman Schoenfeld, private communication (April 23, 1994).

225   **celebrate is Mary Kay Cosmetics:** Alan Farnham, "Mary Kay's Lessons in Leadership," *Fortune* (September 20, 1993), pp. 68–77.

Chapter 16

Page

229   **that is created by failure:** "Make Your Failures Work for You," *Harvard Business Review* (November-December 1993), pp. 11–12.

231 **competitiveness in the world's markets:** David Powis, in association with INSEAD, "Uncommon Courage: New Models of Corporate Leadership," *Business Week* (January 17, 1994), pp. 81–84.

232 **". . . Europe is no longer competitive":** Lewis Finlay, "The Bagnoli Steel Mill Is Empty, Yet a Sign of Hope," *San Diego Union-Tribune,* July 24, 1994, p. I1.

232 **pessimism is prevalent:** Mark Memmott and John Hillkirk, "Japan Inc. Has Lost Aura of Invincibility," *USA Today* (March 3, 1994), pp. B1, B2.

232 **that figure is 19.3 percent:** Lewis Finlay, "Italy's Young Entrepreneurs May Stimulate the Economy," *San Diego Union-Tribune,* July 24, 1994, pp. 1–2.

233 **development of "transcendent importance":** Alfred L. Malabre, "Economy's Slow Place Masks Competitiveness," *The Wall Street Journal* (September 13, 1993), p . A14.

233 **the Americans have won in the competition:** Daniel Strickberger, "The Other American Dream Team," *The Wall Street Journal* (February 15, 1994), p. A14.

233 **created over 18 million net new jobs:** Ibid.

Index